WILLIAM TEMPLE'S
PHILOSOPHY OF RELIGION

WILLIAM TEMPLE'S
PHILOSOPHY OF
RELIGION

by

OWEN C. THOMAS

S·P·C·K

AND

SEABURY PRESS

1961

First published in 1961
by S.P.C.K.
Holy Trinity Church
Marylebone Road
London N.W.1

and The Seabury Press
One Fawcett Place
Greenwich, Connecticut

Made and printed in Great Britain by
William Clowes and Sons, Limited, London and Beccles

To
B.L.T.
A.B.T.   A.L.T.
O.C.T., Jr.

ACKNOWLEDGEMENTS

I WANT to express my gratitude to the Trustees and Faculty of the Episcopal Theological School, Cambridge, Massachusetts, for the opportunity afforded me in 1952–3 to undertake research for this book; to Professors John C. Bennett of Union Theological Seminary, New York, and Horace L. Friess of Columbia University for their guidance and help along the way; and to my colleagues, Professors William J. Wolf and Joseph F. Fletcher, for their encouragement and advice in this project as in all things.

In addition I am grateful to the following publishers for permission to reprint selections from their publications:

Macmillan and Company, Ltd, and St Martin's Press, Inc., for passages from *Mens Creatrix*, *Christ the Truth*, and *Nature, Man and God*, by William Temple; and from *The Nature of Metaphysical Thinking*, by Dorothy M. Emmet.

The Macmillan Company and George Allen and Unwin, Ltd, for passages from *Contemporary British Philosophy: Personal Statements* (First Series), ed. by J. H. Muirhead.

Routledge and Kegan Paul, Ltd, for passages from *Wilhelm Dilthey: An Introduction*, by H. A. Hodges.

The *Anglican Theological Review* for permission to reprint in somewhat different form in Chapter 16 much of the substance of my article, "Reflections on the Philosophy of Religion", Vol. XL (April 1958), pp. 95–107.

Dublin, N.H.   O. C. T.
July 1960

CONTENTS

PART III. APPRAISAL AND RECONSTRUCTION

I

INTRODUCTION AND BACKGROUND

> We have been led to conceive Natural Theology [or the Philosophy of Religion] as that philosophical discipline which pursues enquiries into the true nature and general validity of Religion, making use of the actual religions of mankind to assist it in this enquiry, and setting Religion as a whole, and therefore also each religion in particular, in the context of our knowledge and understanding of the universe.[1]

THUS William Temple, the late Archbishop of Canterbury, defines a subject which has fascinated and baffled men's minds from the beginnings of reflective thought down to the present day. There is perhaps no greater variety in any area of contemporary thought than in that involving religion, philosophy, and theology, and variously referred to as the philosophy of religion, religious philosophy, philosophical theology, or natural theology. The philosophy of religion has received innumerable definitions ranging all the way from the anthropology of religion to something amounting to dogmatic theology.

Furthermore, within the past few decades a "Copernican revolution" has occurred in religious thought which has recast all the traditional problems in such a way that the task of the philosophy of religion has been opened up anew.[2] In this

---

[1] *Nature, Man and God*, p. 28. The publication facts about books and articles by Temple and about Temple referred to in the footnotes are indicated in the Bibliography.

[2] See John A. Hutchison, *Faith, Reason, and Existence: An Introduction to Contemporary Philosophy of Religion* (New York: Oxford University Press, 1956), p. vii.

revolution and in this task the contribution of William Temple has a central place.

Temple holds a unique position among writers on the philosophy of religion in this generation. He was qualified for this by a thorough training in philosophy, a deep and immediate acquaintance with one of the central Christian traditions, and a broad knowledge of ethics, social problems, art, literature, and science. Many ventures in the philosophy of religion have been hampered by a blindness to or lack of sympathy with some major sector of human life, such as aesthetic experience or even religion itself. Temple, however, was clearly a "whole" man such that his thought was not impoverished by blindness to any major aspect of human experience but was marked by an unusual comprehensiveness and coherence.

Moreover, he wrote at the end of an era in British philosophical and theological thought which was actively concerned with the problems of the philosophy of religion. Since that time thought on this subject has tended to be neglected from both the philosophical and the theological sides. It has been neglected from the philosophical side by reducing it to the empirical study of religious phenomena or by considering the philosophical questions raised by religion to be meaningless or outside the purview of philosophy. It has been neglected from the theological side by a denial of the validity of philosophical thought in other than its methodological aspects or by the affirmation that the final formulations in this area were made in a past age. When philosophy and theology return fully to the problems of the philosophy of religion (and the beginnings of such a return are clearly visible to-day), then "the comprehensive grasp and synthetic impulse" of William Temple will be newly appreciated.[1]

In this connection a question may properly be raised about the contemporary significance and importance of the

[1] W. R. Matthews et al., William Temple: An Estimate and An Appreciation, pp. 22f.

contribution to the philosophy of religion of someone whose philosophical background is in Hegelian idealism and to a somewhat lesser extent in the new realism. Many recent philosophical authors have referred to the "philosophical revolution" which has taken place in the last half-century involving a shift from idealism to a radical empiricism, from metaphysics to analysis. It is quite clear that Temple was influenced by this movement in philosophy hardly at all. He knows Moore's work in ethics and Whitehead's in metaphysics and there is one brief reference to Russell's neo-realism in the Gifford Lectures. But there is no evidence of Temple's acquaintance with the movement of logical empiricism or linguistic analysis.

We must conclude, therefore, that Temple's contribution to the philosophy of religion is not directly relevant to the contemporary scene, at least to the larger part of the philosophical side of this scene. But there are signs of a revival of concern with metaphysics and the constructive function of philosophy to-day and in particular with the problems raised for philosophy by various types of religious statement.[1] As this concern develops philosophy must inevitably come to deal again with the problems of the relation of fact and value, of mind and reality, and others which are treated with real insight by William Temple.[2]

Furthermore, what Temple has attempted is the development

[1] See, for example, Stephen Toulmin *et al.*, *Metaphysical Beliefs: Three Essays* (London: S.C.M. Press, 1957); D. F. Pears (ed.), *The Nature of Metaphysics* (New York: St Martin's Press, 1957); Antony Flew and Alasdair MacIntyre (eds.), *New Essays in Philosophical Theology* (New York: The Macmillan Company, 1955); Basil Mitchell (ed.), *Faith and Logic: Oxford Essays in Philosophical Theology* (Boston: The Beacon Press, 1957); Ian T. Ramsey, *Religious Language: An Empirical Placing of Theological Phrases* (London: S.C.M. Press, 1957); Ben F. Kimpel, *Language and Religion: A Semantic Preface to a Philosophy of Religion* (New York: The Philosophical Library, 1957); John Wilson, *Language and Christian Belief* (London: Macmillan and Company, Ltd, 1958).

[2] See, for example, F. H. Cleobury, *Christian Rationalism and Philosophical Analysis* (London: James Clarke and Company, 1959), especially ch. 2, "Linguistic Analysis and Idealism".

of a theistic idealistic metaphysic on the basis of a realistic epistemology. This is of permanent importance philosophically, for as C. D. Broad has asserted:

> The great merit of Idealism is that it really has tried to do justice to the social, ethical, aesthetic and religious facts of the world. The great merit of Realism is that it really has tried to face in a patient and detailed way the problem of matter and of our perception of it. But neither of these activities is a substitute for the other; and a genuine Speculative Philosophy must combine the detailed study of the lower categories with the due recognition of the higher categories, and must try to reconcile the pervasiveness of the former with the apparently growing importance of the latter.[1]

The purpose and scope of this book is the investigation of Temple's thought in so far as it deals with the philosophy of religion broadly interpreted. This will include an analysis and criticism of his basic concepts and categories, an investigation and assessment of the dialectical argument for theism, an appraisal of his work as a whole, and an attempt to draw some conclusions as to the nature of the philosophy of religion and the relation between religion, philosophy, and theology. It will become clear that Temple does not carry out very thoroughly the enterprise defined above and that his concern is more with what will be defined as Christian philosophy or the interpretation of the various realms of experience, including religion, on the basis of Christian theology. An important conclusion of this investigation will be that the philosophy of religion might be more fruitfully defined so as to include the investigation of all world views which function as religions in the life and thought of those who hold them rather than to limit its purview to those world views which have traditionally been called religious.

---

[1] "Critical and Speculative Philosophy", *Contemporary British Philosophy: Personal Statements* (First Series), J. H. Muirhead (ed.) (New York: The Macmillan Company, 1924), p. 99; cf. John Herman Randall, Jr, in *Naturalism and the Human Spirit*, Yervant H. Krikorian (ed.) (New York: Columbia University Press, 1944), pp. 372–6.

In order fully to understand William Temple's contribution to the philosophy of religion it is necessary to see it against the background and in the context of late nineteenth- and early twentieth-century British philosophical and theological thought. Temple's works on the philosophy of religion appeared between the years 1910 and 1944, a period in the history of British philosophy which can be described as one of reaction against certain aspects of the idealistic tradition which held sway in the latter part of the nineteenth century.

Since the Middle Ages the general tendency of western thought had been to find within this world what the medieval man had looked for in another world.[1] This tendency can be seen in the Renaissance, in some aspects of the Reformation, and in the Romantic movement. The philosophical foundations of this immanentism as it appeared especially in the Romantic movement were laid by Spinoza, Kant, Goethe, and Hegel. Although this movement was represented in England by Coleridge before 1850, it made slow headway against the entrenched empiricism and naturalism.

British philosophy of the early nineteenth century was a complex of various strands shaped largely by the tradition of Locke and Hume and their successors. These strands included the Associationist school of James Mill and Thomas Brown, the utilitarianism of Jeremy Bentham and the Mills, the Common Sense philosophy of Thomas Reid and William Hamilton, and the naturalism of Henry Buckle. All these schools understood religion to involve a transcendent object and often questioned the reality of that object.

Until about the middle of the nineteenth century in England philosophical religious thought was not deeply influenced by these empiricist and naturalistic movements. This was due to the fact that, unlike the situation in Germany, there was little fruitful intercourse between philosophers and theologians and each was concerned to emphasize their mutual distinctness.

[1] See Clement C. J. Webb, *A Study of Religious Thought in England from 1850* (Oxford: Basil Blackwell, 1923), p. 21.

As a result philosophical religious thought generally assumed the transcendence of God, creation in time, the revelatory authority of Scripture, and concern for the salvation of individual souls. However, during the second half of the century certain influences combined to modify these assumptions in the direction of a religious immanentism. This immanentism, unlike the empiricism and naturalism mentioned above, would bring the object of religious concern within the immanentist view rather than exclude it. Beside the idea of evolution and the Romantic movement these influences included the rise of a historical sense and the growing prominence of the idealistic philosophy. Since Temple was deeply influenced by British idealism and reacted critically to it, it is necessary to trace the development of this movement and investigate its significance for the philosophy of religion.

The Kantian philosophy and the post-Kantian philosophy of Fichte, Schelling, and Hegel began to influence British philosophy early in the nineteenth century through the attacks upon it by the Associationist and Common Sense schools of James Mill, Brown, and Hamilton and through the thought of Coleridge. J. H. Muirhead says of the latter: "I do not think that there is a point in the Idealism of the 'seventies which was not anticipated, perhaps even better expressed than it has ever been since, by Coleridge in one place or another of his multifarious writings."[1] Coleridge, looking for a metaphysic which would justify the poetic imagination, attacked the empiricism and scepticism of his day with the idealism of Schelling. He was a defender of the traditional creed, although the implications of his philosophy were to modify it radically in an immanentist direction. The more pronounced idealistic immanentism of Thomas Carlyle, Coleridge's younger contemporary, moved further from the traditional creed.

[1] "Past and Present in Contemporary Philosophy", *Contemporary British Philosophy: Personal Statements* (First Series), J. H. Muirhead (ed.), pp. 310f.

The first important work of the new idealist movement was *The Institutes of Metaphysic*, by J. F. Ferrier, published in 1854. However, it was the publication of J. H. Stirling's *The Secret of Hegel* in 1865 which marked the beginning of the real ascendency of idealistic thought in Britain. T. H. Green's introduction to his edition of Hume's *Treatise on Human Nature* (1874) and Edward Caird's *Kant* (1877) began the work of the familiarization of Kant and Hegel in England. The idealism of Green, Caird, F. H. Bradley, and Bernard Bosanquet amounted to a repudiation of the whole British philosophical tradition of empiricism and naturalism. They held that the very existence of art, morality, religion, and science was evidence that reality is more than a collection of facts perceived by the senses and considered in abstraction from the mind. As against empiricism and naturalism the idealists held that the true object of religious faith was to be sought within the world. They were concerned to find within the world of the family, the state, and secular civilization the religious values which had been considered to belong to another world. They emphasized self-realization as the goal of human life, the autonomy of ethics, and the common good as the norm of morality. Thus they rejected both the old supernaturalism and the naturalism which excluded the religious object from this world. Although this position later developed into a denial of any transcendence in religion, the older generation of idealists represented by Green and Caird did not intend to commit themselves to this denial. Green's idealism indeed formed the background of the theology of the celebrated collection of theological essays which appeared in 1889 under the title *Lux Mundi*. Both Green and Caird were able to affirm the immortality of the soul. Their critique of naturalism, their concern with the self-conscious personality and its values, and their view of society as an organism lent themselves to reinterpretations of the traditional doctrines of God, the Incarnation, and the Church which could be considered continuous with the orthodox tradition. The chief

2

concern of the *Lux Mundi* authors was to revive the conception of a self-revelation of the Divine Logos who was immanent in all of the religions of mankind. It is clear that the early idealism was able to supply a basis for this immanentist emphasis.

It soon became clear to some theologians, notably A. S. Pringle-Pattison in his *Hegelianism and Personality* (1886), that the direction of development of idealism tended to deny the personal nature of God and thus any kind of personal relationship with him. God seemed to have become the common element in individual rational and self-conscious minds, the universal of which they were instances. The culmination of this development came in the absolute idealism of Bradley and Bosanquet. Both denied that ultimate reality could be personal in nature, and that the Absolute could be the God who is over against us and with whom we can stand in a personal relation. They also held that personality cannot be the most significant aspect of human nature. By questioning the status of personality in both God and man the absolute idealists cast doubt upon the reality of that relationship between God and man which is the basis of Christianity.

In opposition to these results of the absolute idealism a school of personal idealists arose which received inspiration from Hermann Lotze, who had criticized Hegel at this point. The appearance of this movement was marked by the publication in 1902 of a volume entitled *Personal Idealism*, which included among its contributors G. F. Stout, F. C. S. Schiller, W. R. B. Gibson, and Hastings Rashdall. Although these personal idealists were concerned to affirm as against naturalism the reality of human freedom, the limitations of the evolutionary hypothesis, and the validity of moral evaluation, they considered that "the Absolutist is a more insidious, perhaps more dangerous adversary, just because we seem to have more in common with him".[1] The two points on which they attacked the absolute idealists were the criticism of

[1] Henry Sturt (ed.), *Personal Idealism* (London: Macmillan and Company, Ltd, 1902), p. vii.

human experience from the standpoint of absolute experience rather than from the standpoint of human experience itself and the refusal to recognize adequately the volitional side of human nature. The theological side of this movement was presented by Rashdall and James Martineau.

At about this time Schiller's pragmatism, Ritschl's value theology, and Roman Catholic modernism began to affect philosophical religious thought and lent their weight to the immanentist tendency.

The development of personal idealism marked the beginning of a series of reactions against the prevailing immanentism. The First World War tended to modify this immanentism by casting serious doubt on its generally optimistic view of history and civilization and thus by causing many to turn to the traditional view of a revelation of transcendent values from beyond this world.

The criticism of the naturalistic form of immanentism was carried out by A. J. Balfour, James Ward, F. R. Tennant, and A. E. Taylor. All of these men felt that the naturalistic philosophy failed to make sense not only of the facts of morality, art, religion, and philosophy itself but also of the scientific enterprise from which its principles were derived. They held that these facts of culture and common experience could be coherently interpreted only on the basis of the reality of a transcendent personal God. For this reason they stood apart from the idealist tradition. It is important to note that their philosophy of religion was not a return to the uncritical pre-Kantian proofs but was considered by its propounders to be quite empirical and aware of the latest scientific developments. Furthermore, it had learned much from the idealistic tradition. It was concerned to emphasize the unity of all the various forms of being, the universal immanence of God, and the rejection of the sheer arbitrariness of religion which results from the omission of either of the first two points.

The one other development in British philosophy which is required to complete the picture of the background of Temple's thought is the rise of what has been called the new realism. This is primarily an epistemological movement in reaction to the post-Kantian idealism. It stands for a realistic epistemology and a distrust of system-making in view of the complexity of the details of reality. Some forms included among the independent objects of perception and conception unsubstantial objects such as essences and logical propositions. The movement in England has affinities to the German realism of Brentano and Meinong and the phenomenology of Husserl. The foremost British realists are Bertrand Russell, G. E. Moore, Samuel Alexander, L. T. Hobhouse, and A. N. Whitehead. The influence of this new realism on Temple was mediated primarily by Whitehead.

The philosophical influences on Temple's thought were primarily from the idealist tradition. At the age of sixteen he worked his way through Kant's first *Critique* and the *Metaphysics of Ethics*. At Balliol College, Oxford, he studied under Edward Caird, the teacher who influenced him the most.[1] In the introduction to his Gifford Lectures he states: "Such method in thought as I possess, and especially such grasp of the principles of Dialectic as I have acquired, I believe myself to owe to my Master at Balliol, Edward Caird."[2] Caird inspired him to look on philosophy as the search for a unifying principle in terms of which he might achieve a synthesis of different tendencies of thought. In the introduction to his first systematic work Temple states that the master influences upon his thought were Plato, St John, and Robert Browning.[3] His Platonic studies were always a dominant and pervasive influence.[4] The academic influence of idealism came also through Bradley, Bosanquet, and Josiah Royce. He states that his dialectical method led him to "a position which in its positive content is almost identical with such an idealism as that of

[1] *Thoughts in War-Time*, p. 97.
[2] *Nature, Man and God*, p. x.
[3] *Mens Creatrix*, pp. viif.
[4] See his "Plato's Vision of the Ideas" and *Plato and Christianity*.

Edward Caird or of Bernard Bosanquet, apart from the method of arriving at it".[1] More recently he stated that the books to which he owed most in the forming of his general outlook were Royce's *The World and the Individual* and the Gifford Lectures of Bosanquet, *The Principle of Individuality and Value* and *The Value and Destiny of the Individual*. However, he adds that he never accepted Bosanquet's ultimate position.[2] In his views of the world as apprehended, the relations of the world process, mind, and value, and the structure of the world he is indebted to the realism of Alexander and Whitehead.

In his theology Temple moved steadily in the direction of orthodoxy. After taking his degree at Oxford, he had some years of doubt concerning specific points in the Christian tradition, but in his main theological works he stands in the tradition of liberal catholicism of the authors of *Lux Mundi*. His developed theology is orthodox and conservative but liberal in the sense of accepting the results of the historical disciplines. In the introduction to *Mens Creatrix* he states his indebtedness to the authors of *Concerning Prayer*, who include B. H. Streeter, E. Bevan, L. Hodgson, N. Micklem, and R. G. Collingwood, to Fr Herbert Kelly, s.s.m., and to Charles Gore, the editor of *Lux Mundi*.

W. M. Horton describes Temple as the typical theologian of the moderate or central trend in English theology, as distinguished from the liberal or broad, Anglo-Catholic, and protestant or non-conformist traditions. According to Horton this central party is derived from the "Good Churchmen" led by Bishop Wilberforce who developed out of a group of High Churchmen who refused to join the Tractarian movement and who have been represented by A. C. Headlam, O. C. Quick, and W. R. Matthews.[3]

Temple showed himself to be keenly aware of the rapid

---

[1] *Nature, Man and God*, p. 498.
[2] *Thoughts in War-Time*, p. 97.
[3] *Contemporary English Theology: An American Appreciation* (New York: Harper and Brothers, 1936), pp. 140, 148f.

change in the philosophical and theological atmosphere in the third and fourth decades of this century. In the preface to *Christ the Truth* written in 1924 he stated that the intellectual atmosphere was dominated by a philosophy which was both spiritual and theistic and that a very slight touch to the intellectual balance might incline it towards the possibility of a specific divine incarnation. He believed that philosophically everything was ready for theism and that the construction of a Christocentric metaphysic was now a real possibility.[1] However, in his introduction to *Doctrine in the Church of England* written in 1937 he expressed some doubts as to the possibility of a Christocentric metaphysic and suggested the necessity of moving in the direction of a theology of redemption which admits that much in the world is irrational and unintelligible. In an article in *Theology* written in 1939 he stated his conviction that the statements referred to above in the preface to *Christ the Truth* seemed very remote. He also developed more fully his conviction of the impossibility of a Christian metaphysic which embraces all experience in a coherent and comprehensive scheme.[2]

[1] Cf. *Religious Experience*, p. 80.
[2] Reprinted in *Thoughts in War-Time*, pp. 93–107; cf. "What Christians Stand for in the Secular World", pp. 1f. The development of Temple's thought will be dealt with topically in Part I, especially in the chapters on the structure of reality, logic and dialectic, mind, value, and negative value.

Part I

THE BASIC CONCEPTS

2

METHOD AND NATURAL
THEOLOGY

In all three of his major systematic works Temple's aim is to demonstrate that the Christian hypothesis is adequate to the world, that the Christian faith can best understand and make sense of all the realms of human experience.

In his first major work, *Mens Creatrix*, Temple's method is first to show that the four sciences of knowledge, art, morality, and religion present four converging lines of evidence which do not meet and that this incompleteness threatens their security. Then beginning with the Christian hypothesis he shows that the Incarnation supplies the central point at which the four converging lines meet and find their unity. In the first part he calls his method philosophical; in the second part, theological. The philosophical method is to take the results of all departmental studies and to try to exhibit them as forming a single system. Philosophy has no presuppositions except the validity of reason, the competence of reason to grasp the world as a whole. Philosophy begins with experience and tries to understand and make sense of it.

The theological method begins with faith in the Christian God and attempts to show that God as he has revealed himself is an adequate basis for understanding and making sense of experience. Temple holds that a perfect theology and a perfect philosophy would coincide, philosophy working inward from the circumference and theology out from the centre. Philosophers would discover the Christian God if they could collect the whole universe of facts and reason with perfect cogency concerning them.[1]

[1] *Mens Creatrix*, prologue; cf. *Nature, Man and God*, p. 474.

Temple claims that his method as outlined is broadly scientific. Various fields of data are investigated with the aim of finding a unifying hypothesis. The general lines of a satisfactory hypothesis are thereby determined. Then a positive hypothesis falling within these lines is adopted and tested.[1] Of course, the final hypothesis was held originally by the investigator of the four areas of data, but such presuppositions are unavoidable in the comprehensive philosophical field.

The general method in *Christ the Truth*, Temple's second major systematic work, is similar but more directly theological, and his aim is to present a Christocentric metaphysic. His method is again to deal with the major metaphysical problems, the structure of reality, value, religious experience, man, history, and God, from a philosophical point of view, then to elaborate the central Christian affirmations, and finally to consider the metaphysical problems again in the light of the Christian faith.

Temple's general method in *Nature, Man and God*, is quite different. In the preface he states that his endeavour is "to provide a coherent articulation of an experience which has found some measure of co-ordination through adherence to certain principles".[2] This is described as being in opposition to the method in which each stage is constructed as the basis of the next. However, in an Introductory Note to *Nature, Man and God* Temple refers to the "stages of the argument" which consist of four dialectical transitions beginning with the picture of the world offered by science and concluding with a demand for specific revelation. In the actual elaboration of his method each stage of Temple's argument depends upon the previous one.[3]

In accordance with the terms of the Gifford Trust Temple intends *Nature, Man and God* to be a study in natural theology. He explains, however, that the meaning assigned to this phrase

---

[1] Cf. *The Faith and Modern Thought*, pp. 2ff; *Christianity in Thought and Practice*, pp. 33ff.
[2] P. viii.   [3] See Part II.

by Lord Gifford is no longer tenable and therefore it must be reinterpreted.[1] The original meaning of natural theology as distinguished from revealed theology was such thought about God, the grounds for belief in his existence and certain of his attributes, as might be conducted without reference to the Bible, which was considered to be the repository of the divine self-disclosure and to have final authority in this realm. Revealed theology was thought about God based on his inerrant self-disclosure in the Bible and carried on as a deductive science. Thus it was held that the existence of God was a truth of natural theology and the trinitarian nature of God a truth of revealed theology.

In the nineteenth century the advent of the psychology of religion, anthropology, and the comparative study of religion gave the natural theologian a whole new world of material outside the Bible on which to work. In the same century the advent of the historical critical study of the Bible both made the deductive method of the revealed theologian impossible and opened up another new area for the natural theologian. In other words it became clear that the distinction between natural and revealed theology was not concerned with the content of the material under consideration but solely with the principle determining the method of examination. Specifically, the acceptance of doctrines on the basis of authority lies outside the realm of natural theology, although the doctrine itself and the fact that a particular religious community accepts it on authority are within the purview of natural theology. Indeed the reasonableness and validity of accepting doctrines on authority is a question to be investigated by natural theology.[2]

No element of religion is exempt from examination in natural theology. The task of natural theology is the criticism of religion in the same sense of that word which is used in the aesthetic realm and which is involved in the scientific process.

[1] *Nature, Man and God*, lecture i.
[2] See Chapter 9.

Thus, as we have noted above, Temple defines natural theology as

> that philosophical discipline which pursues enquiries into the
> true nature and general validity of Religion, making use of the
> actual religions of mankind to assist it in this enquiry, and
> setting Religion as a whole, and therefore also each religion in
> particular, in the context of our knowledge and understanding
> of the universe.[1]

It is to include the investigation of the claim of religion to be
the dominant element in man's experience exercising over all
the rest a certain judgement and control.[2] It should be the
criticism of actual religion and actual religious beliefs irre-
spective of their supposed origin and therefore independently
of any supposed act or word of divine revelation, and it
should be conducted with the complete relentlessness of
scientific inquiry.[3] In another context Temple states that "the
method of Natural Theology no doubt requires ideally that
the validity of Religion be established".[4] This would seem to
suggest that it is not within the purview of natural theology to
investigate the general validity of religion, but the opposite is
clearly Temple's meaning as seen in the above references.

Furthermore, if the natural theologian is to know in any
real sense the subject-matter of his study, he must know it
from within by personal participation in one of the religions.[5]
But this raises an acute problem for the natural theologian.
To participate in a particular religion means to be a worshipper, which in turn means the surrender of all faculties to
the object of worship. But this is totally incompatible with
inquiry into the being and attributes of the object of worship;
and it is such critical inquiry which is the essence of natural
theology.

This raises the larger problem of the relation between
natural theology as a philosophical discipline and religion, or

---

[1] *Nature, Man and God*, p. 28.   [2] Ibid., p. 18.   [3] Ibid., p. 27.
[4] Ibid., p. 51.   [5] Ibid., pp. 17, 496.

between natural theology and the systematic elaboration of the doctrines of a particular religion which we may call revealed theology or simply theology.[1] According to Temple the two main factors in the tension between these two disciplines are the identity of province in which each claims supremacy and the opposition in their method of dealing with it resulting from a difference of aim.[2]

The province claimed by both is the entire field of human experience. The resulting tension consists in a sharp difference in temper, mental habit, and outlook with reference to the same objects of attention. "*The primary assurances of Religion are the ultimate questions of philosophy.*"[3] As to aim, philosophy seeks knowledge for the sake of understanding, while theology seeks knowledge for the sake of worship. The aim of the philosopher is to follow the argument wherever it goes; the aim of the theologian is to stabilize and deepen his faith.

The methods of philosophy and theology correspond to their respective attitudes of inquiry and assurance. The method of theology is based on what Temple describes as the three central convictions of religion in its higher forms: namely, spirit is a true source of initiation of processes, all existence finds its source in a supreme spiritual reality, and between that spirit and ourselves there can be true fellowship.[4] It might have been simpler had Temple limited himself explicitly to the Hebrew–Christian tradition, because many would dispute the description of these particular convictions as "higher".

The method of theology takes its start from the conviction of the existence of such a supreme spirit and seeks to offer explanations of the facts of experience by reference to the character of the supreme spirit; that is, theology attempts to account for everything by the highest category of all. Philosophy (and therefore natural theology), on the other hand, starts from the detailed experience of men and seeks to build

---

[1] Temple refers to them as "Philosophy" and "Religion" in lecture ii of *Nature, Man and God*.

[2] Ibid., pp. 30ff.   [3] Ibid., p. 35.   [4] Ibid., p. 35.

up its understanding of that experience by reference to it alone. Philosophy because of its kinship with science attempts to account for everything by the lowest category possible. Temple gives as an example the interpretation of psychological data. The psychologist as a scientist must exhaust all possibilities of a purely psychological origin of religious convictions before admitting the hypothesis of action upon the human mind by God, a being necessarily unknown to the psychologist as scientist.

Temple suggests certain principles by which the tension between philosophy and theology may be reduced to that which is inevitable and necessary and by which tensions due to misapprehension of the methods and aims of philosophy and theology may be avoided. The theologian must distinguish between the elements or expressions of his faith which are essential and those which are unessential. The philosopher must realize that he is entitled to see how far he can go without the higher categories, but that he is not entitled to deny the applicability of them, unless they should deny the philosophical method. Furthermore, the philosopher must realize that there are spheres in which the characteristic methods of science are inapplicable, such as ethics, aesthetics, and personal relations. Here Temple means that our appreciation of value is independent of argument and experiment, and he quotes F. H. Bradley: "Our sense of value, and in the end for every man his own sense of value, is ultimate and final."[1]

Thus, the natural theologian who attempts personally to bridge these tensions between philosophy and theology, to combine the attitudes of inquiry and assurance and their correlative methods, can only do so by a deliberate alternation of attention. Temple points out later that this problem is simplified in the case of Christians because the fullest practice of Christianity requires the complete operation of both attitudes.[2]

[1] *Essays on Truth and Reality*, p. 132; quoted in *Nature, Man and God*, p. 53.
[2] Ibid., pp. 44, 496f.

3

THE STRUCTURE OF REALITY

TEMPLE'S view of the structure of reality includes a basic metaphysical presupposition concerning reality as a whole and an analysis of the nature of the structure of reality. Both are of central importance for his view of epistemology and thus for his dialectical argument for theism.

Temple's basic metaphysical presupposition as to the structure of reality is that the universe is a rational whole or unity. This presupposition takes different forms in his successive works. It has two aspects which are related: that the universe is rational and that it is a unity. He holds that this is a necessary presupposition of both science and philosophy. Science assumes that the world is rational in the sense that when you have thought through the implications of your experience, the result is fact. Our experience is assumed to be rationally coherent according to discoverable principles.[1] In other words, when mind is true to itself, it reaches its truest apprehension of reality.[2]

Temple quotes Balfour to the effect that scientists have always been restive under a multiplication of entities, and that there is no *a priori* reason for this, only that it is more satisfying to the intellect. Thus, the basis of all science is the assumption that the truth about facts is what satisfies the mind of man, that those principles which govern our thinking exist in the real world.[3] For example, we cannot say, if two plus

---

[1] *The Faith and Modern Thought*, pp. 9f.
[2] *Nature, Man and God*, p. 148.
[3] *The Faith and Modern Thought*, pp. 12f.

two equals four, then two apples plus two apples equals four apples, unless we assume that the principles of reasoning are valid for the real world. The rationality of the universe is an act of faith, but it is the primary certainty upon which all other certainty depends.[1] Approaching this in another way Temple states that since knowledge is one of the facts which must be held together in the coherent scheme assumed by science and philosophy, "there is some mentality . . . in all the facts of our experience. . . . Everything which exists must be the embodiment of rational principle. The Universe turns out to be a rational whole."[2]

This introduces the second aspect of the basic metaphysical presupposition which is based on the dictum of Plato that "nature is all of it akin".[3] Science sets out with an ideal of knowledge before it, a coherent and comprehensive statement of the whole field of fact. Reason demands that the world shall be regarded as coherent, as making up one system, although there is no ground in experience for postulating this.[4] Logically stated, the subject of every judgement is reality as a whole. In all scientific thought there must be an explicit or implicit reference to the system of reality as a whole.[5]

Approaching this basic presupposition philosophically Temple states that the only presupposition of philosophy is "the validity of reason (or, to put it otherwise, the rationality of the universe). Philosophy assumes the competence of reason . . . to grasp the world as a whole."[6] We have to choose between postulating a rational universe and accepting complete scepticism.[7] Philosophy presupposes that the universe is a single system, no part of which can be wholly un-

[1] *Mens Creatrix*, p. 89.

[2] *The Faith and Modern Thought*, p. 11.

[3] *Meno*, 81 c. Cf. Temple's comment on this in *Plato and Christianity*, pp. 12f.

[4] *The Faith and Modern Thought*, pp. 2f.

[5] *Mens Creatrix*, pp. 55f.

[6] Ibid., p. 2.

[7] *Christ the Truth*, p. 10.

connected with any other part.[1] The goal of philosophy is to
grasp the whole universe as a nexus of relations.[2]

In later works, Temple speaks of this presupposition in
more empirical terms. There is a kinship or correlation between mind and the world which it apprehends Mind finds
what is akin to itself in its object when it studies the world.[3]
This is an experience which has two aspects. First, mind finds
the counterpart of the principle of its own activities, e.g., the
mathematical properties of mechanical combinations of forces
or of aesthetic proportions. Second, with this discovery goes a
feeling of being at home with the object.[4]

This basic metaphysical presupposition affects all of
Temple's arguments for theism. If the truth about facts is
what satisfies the mind of man, then since the concept of
purpose is a satisfactory answer to the problem of an explanation for the existence of the universe, it may be the true explanation.[5] The fact that the world process gives rise to minds
which are akin to the process, i.e., find their own principles in
the process, indicates that the ground of the process must involve
mind. Thus mind becomes the principle of unity of the process.
The implication of these conclusions is immanent theism.[6]

In his latest writings Temple gives up this metaphysical
presupposition of the rationality of the universe under the
influence of the process philosophy and his deep awareness of
the disruptions of modern life. In 1937 he stated that his
thought was moving more toward a theology of redemption
which admits that much in the world is irrational and unintelligible.[7] In 1939 he wrote that no Christian map of the
world could be made, that there was much of which no sense

---

[1] *The Nature of Personality*, pp. 82f; *Mens Creatrix*, p. 55; *Nature, Man and God*, p. 504.
[2] *Mens Creatrix*, p. 71; cf. also pp. 1, 22, 23, 59, 85, 175, 255, 353.
[3] See Chapter 6.
[4] *Nature, Man and God*, pp. 129f, 148f, 165.
[5] *The Faith and Modern Thought*, p. 14; *Mens Creatrix*, pp. 258, 353.
[6] *Nature, Man and God*, pp. 129ff, 217ff. See Chapter 11.
[7] *Doctrine in the Church of England*, p. 17.

3

could be made.[1] In 1942 he stated: "What we must get completely away from is the notion that the world as it now exists is a rational whole. . . . The world as we see it is strictly unintelligible."[2] He points out, however, that this falls formally within his earlier interpretation and is implied in the treatment of the problem of evil in his earlier works where he states that evil is only justified when overcome.[3] Furthermore, Temple asserts that this is not a substantial modification in his thought but rather a change of emphasis and that the elaboration of a Christocentric metaphysic or a Christian map of life is a permanent need and the supreme task of theology in all ages.

Temple's analysis of the actual structure of reality is empirical, and he considered it to be the view of modern science. The structure of the world consists of a scale of being, a series of strata, levels, degrees, or grades of reality. This scale is described as matter, life, mind, and spirit, or thing, brute, and person, or inorganic matter, organic matter, vegetable life, animal life, and personality. These stages are described as entities or modes of action and reaction. However, they are abstractions from a continuous scale. Furthermore, such a scale should not imply that some stages exist more genuinely than others.

In this scale each stage depends for its existence upon those below it and each is completed, fulfilled, and reveals its full potentialities only in so far as it is possessed, indwelt, or controlled by that above it. The lower stage is necessary to the activity of the higher, but the lower only finds its fullness of being when it is used by the higher as its means of self-realization. The scale is marked by an increasing development of sentience, self-determination, self-motion, an individual point of view, and ability to respond to environment. There is an increasing recalcitrance to generalized treatment, that is,

[1] *Thoughts in War-Time*, pp. 101, 106.

[2] From a letter to D. Emmet; quoted in F. A. Iremonger, *William Temple, Archbishop of Canterbury: His Life and Letters*, pp. 537f.

[3] *Thoughts in War-Time*, pp. 99, 102, 107; *Doctrine in the Church of England*, p. 17; Iremonger, op. cit., pp. 537f.

individuality becomes more and more important in relation to generic qualities. Time becomes increasingly significant to the various stages in the scale. In each stage new qualities appear which are not deducible from the lower stages.

Matter or thing covers the substances or modes of action and reaction which are studied in the sciences of physics and chemistry. It has no point of view to consider, is insentient, and makes no claims upon us. Other objects are without value or significance for it. It is moved only from without and its individuality is negligible. It reveals its full potentialities only when informed and controlled by life.

Life in its vegetable form has more individuality and to some extent determines its reactions to its environment in the beginnings of self-motion. Animal life has subjectivity, sentience, and a point of view to be considered, but its subjectivity is limited to feeling and to the present. There is a higher degree of self-motion, a richer variety of modes of reaction to the environment, and increased individuality. Life reveals its full potentialities only when it is indwelt or possessed by mind. Animal life in its higher forms involves mind or the capacity for calculation of means to ends presented as good. Mind, in turn, reaches its full actualization only when it is indwelt and controlled by spirit or personality.

Spirit or personality is found only in human beings and is distinguished by consciousness of continued existence and concern with the past and the future as well as the present. Here individuality is at least as important as generic qualities. Personality is the subject of rights and duties, of obligation or ultimate value. It is marked by freedom, responsibility, character, and purpose. It has the capacity for forming ideals and participating in communal life. It has the capacity of choosing between ends by reference to an ideal standard of good.[1]

---

[1] *The Nature of Personality*, pp. 3–8, 15–21; "Some Implications of Theism", pp. 418f; *Christ the Truth*, pp. 4–7, 59ff; *Christian Faith and Life*, pp. 14f; *Nature, Man and God*, pp. 121f, 190n, 474ff; *Christianity in Thought and Practice*, pp. 54ff; *Religious Experience*, pp. 77f. Temple refers to a fuller treatment in L. S. Thornton, *The Incarnate Lord*, ch. ii.

Although from the point of view of science it is not clear whether there are highest or lowest terms in this scale, Temple goes on to suggest that the ideal limit of the scale would be a spiritual being who is completely self-determined, to whom all time has value and therefore is present, who is always guided by his whole purpose, and who is absolutely free. When possessed and controlled by such a being, spirit or personality reveals its full potentialities.[1]

Temple makes use of this view of strata or degrees of reality in his arguments for theism. The picture of reality as existing in levels suggests that the universe must be interpreted by spiritual rather than by mechanical or other materialistic categories. Also spirit or personality, the highest level in the scale of being, involves the capacity for purpose, and this offers a possible explanation of the existence of the universe.[2] "In so far as the universe is a single system, its 'highest principle of unity' must be sought in spirit", because where spirit exists it exercises control.[3] Thus the principle involved in the scientific view of the structure of reality may be the principle of reality as a whole.[4]

---

[1] *The Nature of Personality*, pp. 17, 78ff; *Christ the Truth*, pp. 4f.

[2] *The Nature of Personality*, pp. 85f, 93f; *Mens Creatrix*, p. 258; "Some Implications of Theism", p. 418; *Christ the Truth*, pp. 7f; *Christian Faith and Life*, pp. 13f.

[3] *Nature, Man and God*, p. 479.

[4] "Some Implications of Theism", pp. 418f; *Christian Faith and Life*, p. 15; *Nature, Man and God*, pp. 479f; *Christianity in Thought and Practice*, pp. 56, 71f.

4

LOGIC AND DIALECTIC

SINCE there has been a minimum of agreement in the history of western thought as to the nature and function of logic, a thinker's views on this subject will be especially revealing of his basic presuppositions. Temple's treatment of logic is deeply influenced by Bosanquet and Bradley. It consists of a criticism of the traditional logic and a plea for a new understanding of the nature and function of logic.

According to Temple's preliminary definition logic is the science of intellectual process so far as this leads to knowledge. It is the method of the will to know, the impulse towards totality in the intellectual sphere.[1] Thus, logic is not a special or independent science but the science or art of dealing appropriately with the subject-matter of the various areas of study. Since it is the study of the validity of mental processes, the autonomy of logic must be presupposed by every science.[2]

Temple assents to the summary criticism of the traditional logic that deduction has no right to its starting-point and induction no right to its conclusion. In short, traditional logic is of rhetorical value only.[3] But his criticism is more thoroughgoing than this. The trouble with deduction is in the major premise. In the first place, there are valid syllogisms which have no major premise. Furthermore, the universal which is the major premise of the standard deductive syllogism can be reached by enumeration or it can be treated as a definition.

[1] *Mens Creatrix*, pp. 10, 12, 30, 65.
[2] *Nature, Man and God*, pp. xviii, 33.
[3] *Mens Creatrix*, p. 15; *Studies in the Spirit and Truth of Christianity*, p. 42; *Nature, Man and God*, p. 90.

Enumeration is seldom applicable, and when it is, no inference is necessary, since the enumeration must have included the fact stated in the conclusion. If the major premise is a generic judgement, it becomes a definition, and it can be referred to experience only hypothetically.[1] Because of the mathematical character of deductive logic, it is indifferent and therefore inadequate to time and process and thus to our apprehension of the phenomenal and historical world.[2] Finally, the deductive method of thought historically has been inelastic and inadequate to deal with new facts and considerations. Temple points out that the medieval scholastic synthesis was so complete that when new experience was intruded the system was completely shattered. An example of this is the difficulty with the doctrine of real kinds which affirms that there are distinct and unchanging universals upon which inference can safely be based. The development of biological evolution has destroyed this concept.[3]

Temple believes that induction as elaborated by Mill, for example, can never offer certainty in its conclusions, because it requires the impossible task of listing all the possibilities and disproving all but one. Furthermore, our premises or assumptions in induction will determine the nature of the facts observed, and every observation of fact will modify the original assumptions. It is impossible to build on the facts, because, until the structure is complete, their nature is not fully known.[4] If it is objected that Aristotle's description of how knowledge is obtained at the end of the *Posterior Analytics* is a presentation of induction which takes these objections into account, Temple's reply is that this is not formal inductive logic but a description of living thought.[5]

---

[1] *Mens Creatrix*, pp. 12f; *Nature, Man and God*, pp. 89f.
[2] *Nature, Man and God*, pp. 87f.
[3] *Mens Creatrix*, p. 13; *Nature, Man and God*, p. 102; *Christianity in Thought and Practice*, p. 18.
[4] *Mens Creatrix*, pp. 15f; *Christianity in Thought and Practice*, p. 15.
[5] *Nature, Man and God*, pp. 93f.

For the reasons given above, Temple believes that the traditional logic is incapable of dealing with historical and individual reality. This incapacity derives from its basis in mathematics. Because traditional logic is a special application of the principles of mathematics, it is involved in the limitation of mathematics that although it tells us something about everything, it tells us very little about anything. As a result traditional logic is valuable as having complete validity in relation to certain types of argument, as supplying a norm for cogency in all types of argument, as a standard of reference and norm of procedure, and as an extremely valuable preparatory discipline, but not as a universal guide to valid thinking.[1] It is on the basis of these criticisms of formal logic that Temple offers his suggestions as to the nature and function of logic.

Temple describes his alternative proposal for logical method as circular, artistic, critical, and dialectical. All living thought proceeds in circles or pendulum-swings. A group of facts suggests a theory which brings a fuller grasp of the facts, which in turn modifies the theory, and so forth. This results not in a universal proposition with which deduction can begin but in a whole system, a concrete universal, in which each element has its place. Temple quotes Caird as saying: "There is no harm in arguing in a circle if the circle is large enough."[2] Thus living circular thought moves around a system of facts improving its understanding of the system and its constituent parts at every stage. If this kind of thought can be called inference, then the middle term is the system as a whole, not an abstract quality or a fixed genus but a concrete universal. Thus, all valid argument is circular and the circle must include the whole universe.[3]

Temple puts this another way by stating that living thought is always both deductive and inductive at the same time. In

[1] Ibid., pp. 13, 47, 87f, 106f.

[2] *Studies in the Spirit and Truth of Christianity*, p. 42; "Some Implications of Theism", pp. 416f; *Nature, Man and God*, p. 147.

[3] *Mens Creatrix*, p. 17; *Christianity in Thought and Practice*, pp. 21f.

the beginning the group of facts under consideration suggests some kind of system or theory. Further study of the facts modifies the system. The modified system suggests new aspects of the facts to be examined. In the earlier phase the method is predominantly inductive; in the later, deductive. Generalization and apprehension of particulars must interact. Thus, the method will be "the progressive systematization of our experience as we apprehend it".[1] The different kinds of inference describe passing phases of the activity of thought. As a result thought will not be faced with dilemmas over whether reality is one or many but will investigate how reality is one and how it is many.[2]

As is clear from the above survey, although Temple rejects the traditional logic, he still holds that the universal is the key to cogent reasoning. However, since evolution has made belief in distinct and unalterable real kinds impossible, Temple has substituted the concrete universal. He considers the method of the concrete universal to be a development of the method described at the end of the *Posterior Analytics*, and he believes that it is the distinctive contribution of modern thought to logic.[3]

Temple holds that the judgement is the unit and the whole of thought, and the necessary element in any judgement is the universal. The crucial problem concerning the universal is its relation to the individual. Plato recognized the problem in his teaching about the realm of phenomena between being and non-being; Aristotle in his teaching about matter. But the scholastic logic avoided the problem, and modern science had to part company with it in order to deal with the individuality of the extant thing. This cleavage between logic and science continued until by means of the idea of evolution it became possible to replace the idea of the determining activity of the generic concept with the idea of the development of the species through actual generations. Thus, "the

---

[1] *Mens Creatrix*, p. 20.   [2] Ibid., pp. 15–22.
[3] Ibid., p. 13; *Nature, Man and God*, pp. 96f.

race which develops is the concrete universal which needs no
ontological argument to add concreteness to it".[1] Temple
believes that this suggestion goes a long way towards overcoming the division between the universal and the individual,
but still the generic character of the race does not completely
pervade and interpenetrate its members. The best example
of the concrete universal is the historical individual, not as a
person but such an entity as the British Empire, the Renaissance, or the Reformation.[2]

Thus, the judgement becomes "the articulation of a system,
the realization of the concrete universal or unity as a whole
of parts or as a principle operative in divers modes".[3] At the
beginning of the investigation a universal will be more
abstract than a concrete particular. At the end of the investigation, however, the universal will be concrete in regard to
relevant qualities while the particular will be relatively
abstract. In this context inference becomes the apprehension
of the relation between two or more of the differences inherent in some one universal or system. Thus, the comprehensive intellectual method can be described as "the ever
fuller apprehension of the concrete universal which is the
same thing as the ever wider grasp and closer correlation of
the facts of experience".[4]

The problem of the relation of the universal and the particular leads to Temple's statement that the artistic element
is a necessary part of the intellectual method. The intellect
can assert that universal and particular are complementary
aspects of an identity, but this is merely formal. The mind cannot realize the identity of the universal and particular without passing from the scientific method to the artistic method.
For example, the characters in a drama are the union of
universal and particular. Thus, after an analysis of the relation

[1] Michael Foster, *Mind*, N.S. CLVII (January 1931), 17; quoted by
Temple, *Nature, Man and God*, p. 100.
[2] Ibid., pp. 98–100.
[3] *Mens Creatrix*, p. 62.   [4] Ibid., p. 65.

of intellect and imagination, Temple can say, "Art is, in structure, Logic *in excelsis*".[1] The scientific intellect leads to a non-temporal understanding of an object known to be successive; imagination leads beyond an escape from the temporal to a mastery and comprehension of time. Furthermore, since logical content cannot exist without mental image or symbol, a main function of art is to supply adequate imagery for concepts. Finally, because the scientific intellect attends only to the universal aspect or meaning of a fact, the "such", it is necessarily abstract and ignores a part of the reality, namely, the "this". The scientific intellect can never fully grasp its own subject matter because of its initial act of abstraction. Only art can know the "this", the concrete particularity, adequately, and therefore art is a necessary complement to science in gaining knowledge of reality.[2]

It is in his later works that Temple describes his logical method as critical and dialectical, in reference to Kant and Plato. Temple believes that, although Kant continues the Cartesian error in epistemology, in devising the critical method he has developed the proper instrument for philosophy and therefore for natural theology. The Cartesian philosophers had discarded the scholastic logic without providing a substitute. They trusted in the natural light of reason without developing a new discipline of accurate and valid thought. Kant's critical method is the true substitute for the scholastic logic. This method which is neither deductive nor inductive begins by investigating the conditions of experience in general to ascertain the principles presupposed in its possibility. For example, by the process called transcendental deduction it is determined that the universality of causation is not an inductive inference from the observation of sequences, but it is a presupposition of all rational experience.

This Kantian critical method overcomes a major difficulty

---

[1] *Mens Creatrix*, p. 154.
[2] Ibid., pp. 39–43, 71f, 154f.

of the traditional logic in that it is able in principle to deal with process, because Kant understood that the mental act which is the ground of validity of a conclusion is mediated and conditioned. Hegel developed this in the study of the dialectical process.[1] As it actually works out, Temple's method is critical only in the general sense of inquiring what is involved in the assumptions commonly held. Thus, the method in the Gifford Lectures is to discover what is implied in the assumption of a realistic epistemology.

In describing his logical method as dialectical Temple apparently means no more than to associate himself with the method of Plato as exemplified in the central books of the *Republic*. Every truth is only a partial truth, and we must seek the contexts in which it appears false in order to correct and develop it. Alleged facts or widely held beliefs are not rejected because they do not harmonize with a theory held, but they are tested and used to develop the theory so that it may be truer to reality. In other words, because logical thought cannot affirm contradiction, it is contradiction which is the stimulus to logical thought. Thought finds incoherence in its apprehension and reorganizes its content in order to remove the incoherence and attain a more inclusive systematic apprehension.[2]

Temple believes that the Hegelian dialectic cannot be an adequate guide for the actual thinking of an individual philosopher, unless the subject matter be an historical era, a movement of thought over an extended period. Any other subject matter would have to be highly abstract or else too limited in scope to be a topic for philosophical discussion.

In the dialectical system the thesis formulates a prima facie view which has much of the quality of common sense, the direct unsophisticated deposit of actual experience. The antithesis, which is usually historically briefer than the other two,

---

[1] *Nature, Man and God*, pp. 74f, 104f; *Christianity in Thought and Practice*, pp. 19f.

[2] *Mens Creatrix*, p. 66; *Christianity in Thought and Practice*, pp. 19f.

is derived from the limitations of the thesis, the aspects of the problem which it neglects. The affirmation of these aspects cannot be comprehended by the thesis, and a new start is required. The antithesis which is thus stated is usually artificial, consciously constructed, and less profound in comparison to the thesis. When the antithesis has been fully elaborated and its shortcomings become apparent, the time has arrived for the synthesis. This is not merely an average between the thesis and the antithesis. It is a reassertion of the thesis with all which has been proven valid in the antithesis incorporated into it.[1]

Temple gives various examples of dialectical movements of thought. The parliamentary history of Great Britain under the two party system shows a dialectical development from the old Conservative party through the Liberal party to the new Conservative party. The history of political organization shows a dialectical development from communism through various affirmations of individualism to a collectivism.[2]

It is because of this understanding of his method that Temple once thought of sub-titling his Gifford Lectures "A Study in Dialectical Realism" thus signifying his aim to make some contribution toward "a dialectic more comprehensive in its range of apprehension and more thorough in its appreciation of the inter-play of factors in the real world" than the dialectical materialism of Marx, Engels, and Lenin, which he felt has so strong an appeal to the contemporary mind and so strong a foundation in contemporary experience.[3] Temple is in agreement with dialectical materialism in its affirmation of the priority of matter, its regarding mind as appearing in matter but not identical with matter, its assertion that mind acts by its own principles which are not reducible to the categories of physics and chemistry. Temple believes, however, that dialectical materialism is not thoroughly dialectical

---

[1] *Nature, Man and God*, pp. 57ff.
[2] Ibid., p. 59; *Mens Creatrix*, pp. 66f.
[3] *Nature, Man and God*, pp. ixf.

at this point. It limits the activity of mind to reaction to situations presented by the material order so that mind is always secondary and dependent. In opposition to this view Temple describes mind as having free ideas and therefore as being predominant in the world.[1]

The main dialectical movement of thought with which Temple is concerned, especially in the Gifford Lectures, is that whose thesis is the realistic epistemology of ancient and medieval thought, whose antithesis is the Lutheran and Cartesian movement leading to an idealistic epistemology, and whose synthesis is the dialectical realism to which Temple hopes he may contribute.[2] The principle of the thesis is that in experience we are directly aware of real objects. This was held, sometimes critically as in Plato and sometimes un-critically, from Thales to Occam. The Sophists represent a small antithesis which was soon swallowed up in the main thesis. Medieval realism was not set over against idealism but against nominalism and conceptualism. The argument was not over the relation of the mind to real objects but over the question whether certain ideas are ideas of real objects. That we have knowledge of real objects was not disputed. The final form of the thesis came in the middle ages with the universal Church and the magnificently coherent scheme of thought embracing theology, metaphysics, logic, politics, ethics, and economics.

Temple believes that the antithesis developed in the fifteenth century. The rising critical spirit, the developing nationalism, and the new Greek learning led to the development of the primary principle of the antithesis, namely, the principle of private judgement. Although the heralding of the antithesis came first in the political sphere in the works of Machiavelli, the first real breach of the thesis came with Luther's stand at the Diet of Worms. The philosophical analogue came in

[1] Ibid., pp. 488, 498. See Chapters 5 and 8.
[2] Ibid., pp. 60ff, 75ff, 404f; *Christianity in Thought and Practice*, pp. 43f; *Religious Experience*, pp. 97ff.

Descartes' meditations in the stove-heated room. The principle of the antithesis took the form of individualism in the Renaissance and Reformation. Dependence upon the universal system was replaced by a resort to the individual conscience and mind. The primary principle took the form of the obligation upon every rational intelligence to master his own experience as fully as possible. The destruction of the thesis resulted in the departmentalization of life which meant the emancipation of cultural activities and greater thoroughness in the study of the facts but also the disruption of the various areas of life. Machiavelli's declaration of the independence of politics led to the fuller development of national cultures but also to national self-assertion and war. Luther's affirmation of the ultimacy of the individual conscience in religion led to a new emphasis on the personal element in religion but tended to cut it off from the other realms of life. The similar emancipation of art led to an enrichment of all forms but also to a destructive detachment and ingrownness.

Philosophy emancipated by Descartes' experiment in universal doubt, was freed to organize experience autonomously but has been largely occupied with the inquiry as to whether and how knowledge is possible at all. Science and politics were forced to get on with the business of the world and leave philosophy to play with its epistemological riddles.

Temple believes that philosophy since Descartes has suffered from "the inherent error of its initial assumption that in knowledge the mind begins with itself and proceeds to the apprehension of the external world by way of construction and inference".[1] This is the error which went along with the positive principle of individual judgement of the antithesis. The repudiation of this error and the current rise of neo-Thomism mark the end of the philosophic era of the antithesis and set the stage for the development of a new synthesis. (In his view that the modern period in philosophy is at an end,

---

[1] *Nature, Man and God*, p. 73.

Temple is in agreement with Whitehead.)[1] Temple claims that one of the first to make this repudiation was Baron von Hügel in *The Reality of God*, written in 1924 and published posthumously in 1931.[2]

The overcoming of the error of the antithesis must be in the return to the concrete richness and bewildering variety and interconnection of actual experience. Although the synthesis will resemble the thesis more than the antithesis, it must not be a simple return to the Middle Ages, because the positive principle of the antithesis must be incorporated into the synthesis. We cannot go behind the discovery and affirmation of the obligation of private judgement, the autonomy of the individual conscience, and the integrity of the individual mind which were affirmed in the antithesis.

The task of constructing the synthesis is one of incorporating the positive gains of the last four centuries into a reconstituted unity of articulated experience. Temple claims that "the restoration of unity to man's experience depends mainly on securing at once the supremacy of Religion among human interests, and the true spirituality of Religion both in itself and in the mode of its supremacy".[3] Apparently it is the aim of the Gifford Lectures to support this claim.

Besides considering his whole work as an attempt to suggest a dialectical synthesis, Temple also describes his Gifford Lectures in an Introductory Note as a series of four dialectical transitions. This seems out of accord with his statement that dialectic cannot successfully be used as a guide for the actual thinking of an individual philosopher. Part II will be devoted to an analysis of this dialectical argument. Let it merely be noted here that the above-mentioned Introductory Note seems to have been added as an afterthought, because there is no explicit mention of a dialectical method in the body of the argument.

[1] *Adventures of Ideas*, ch. x; referred to, *Nature, Man and God*, p. 405n.
[2] Quoted, *Nature, Man and God*, pp. 78f.
[3] Ibid., p. 81; cf. A. E. Baker (ed.), *William Temple's Teaching*, pp. 17ff.

If Temple describes his logical method as circular, artistic, critical, and dialectical, what is the content of this method? What is his final definition of logic? We need logic, he states, to aid us in our estimate of our approximations to valid thought or true knowledge, to aid us in discriminating between degrees of probability and between degrees of justification attaching to unproved assurances.[1] Since the understanding of all existing things is to be reached in part by the study of the historical process which has produced them, the understanding and evaluation of thought is to be reached by a study of the history of thought. Thus, Temple concludes that "the discipline required to perform the function traditionally ascribed to Logic is the History of Thought and especially the History of Philosophy".[2] If logic is to be considered the discipline which results in accurate and adequate thinking, then the only relevant meaning the word can have is that meaning which is implied in the phrase "the logic of the situation" when used in a non-metaphorical sense. Temple here associates himself with Bosanquet who describes logic as "the spirit of totality", and states: "By logic we understand, with Plato and Hegel, the supreme law or nature of experience, the impulse towards unity and coherence (the positive spirit of non-contradiction) by which every fragment yearns toward the whole to which it belongs." "All logical activity is a world of content reshaping itself by its own laws in presence of new suggestions; a syllogism is in principle nothing less, and a Parthenon or *Paradise Lost* is in principle nothing more."[3]

In Temple's discussions of these problems there seems to be some confusion between logic and logical method. He states that his logical method is not deductive or inductive but

---

[1] *Nature, Man and God*, pp. 84, 105.

[2] Ibid., p. 106; cf. p. 497. J. V. L. Casserley has made a similar suggestion in his idea of the "logic of the singular" or "historical logic", *The Christian in Philosophy* (London: Faber and Faber, 1949), p. 194; cf. pp. 31f, 217, 242f.

[3] *The Principle of Individuality and Value*, pp. 23, 333, 340; quoted, *Nature, Man and God*, p. 108.

circular, artistic, critical, and dialectical. But he also states that the discipline which can best perform the function traditionally attributed to logic is the study of the history of thought. Furthermore, he presents as the most fruitful definition of logic, the spirit of totality. It is difficult to see how these three statements can be reconciled. It may be that the application of what is learned in the study of the history of thought to philosophical problems amounts to the application of the dialectical method. This is generally what Temple is doing in seeing his task as the construction of a synthesis of the ancient and medieval thesis and the Lutheran and Cartesian antithesis. Furthermore, his method in all three systematic works seems to be one in which the history of thought plays a considerable part. Terms, problems, and conclusions are analysed from the point of view of their historical context and development. It is not clear, however, how such a logical method is related to the broad definition of logic adopted from Bosanquet.

Temple's logical views are a statement of his philosophical method. Since the philosophy of religion or natural theology is a department of philosophy, the logic supplies the method for this discipline as well. Thus by means of the dialectical method the nature and validity of religion is to be examined.

5

EPISTEMOLOGY

TEMPLE'S treatment of epistemology is a basic part of his philosophy of religion. It is the basis not only of his theory of religious experience and religious knowledge but also of his dialectical argument for theism in the Gifford Lectures. Although he nowhere specifically defines it, Temple understands by epistemology the analysis of the knowledge process, of the subject-object relationship, or of the relation of the mind to its objects. Temple's consideration of epistemology consists primarily of a criticism of Cartesian and idealistic theories and the presentation of a realistic or organic theory.[1] This is part of his projected presentation of a synthesis of the modern antithesis to the ancient-medieval thesis.

Temple considers the day which Descartes spent "shut up alone in a stove-heated room" in Germany as the most disastrous moment in the history of Europe and especially in the history of European philosophy. He considers Descartes' method of universal doubt as logically invalid. It is true that one cannot doubt that he doubts, but it is also true that one cannot really doubt all else but oneself. Temple believes that he himself does not have any greater psychological assurance about his own existence than he does about the existence of a great deal else. He holds that Descartes' argument is based on the possibility of the isolation of the subjective function of thought from all objects of thought. The subjective function of thought can be distinguished from every object of thought taken separately, but it cannot be isolated from all objects of

---

[1] See *Nature, Man and God*, lectures iii and v, respectively.

thought without ceasing to exist. All thought must be about something, either a percept or an image.[1] Thus, Descartes' assurance is psychological rather than logical. He could not refute the suggestion that he is a figure in the dream of a Demiurge who dreamed of him as being sure of his own existence. Descartes' presumed feeling that he is not a figure in such a dream is an assurance of the same kind which Temple has of the existence of other things besides himself. The assurance of one's own existence arises together with the assurance of the existence of other things; they are different elements in the initial fact of consciousness. Temple believes that he can entertain the possibility that all experience and existence is the dream of a Demiurge without intellectual turmoil. But he cannot contemplate the hypothesis that his primary assurance is of his own existence and that his awareness of the world about him is secondary and derivative "without intellectual perturbation of the profoundest kind—a perturbation which is the deposit of all the acrobatic feats by which philosophers from Descartes to Kant have worked out the implications of that hypothesis and tried to avoid becoming entangled by it in manifest nonsense".[2]

Descartes' doubt was really an artificial or academic doubt, and he had as good ground for doubting everything as anything. He was really as sure of the stove-heated room as of himself. If it be argued that his doubt was not an empirical absence of assurance but an ideal supposal, Temple replies that the method may be permissible but that Descartes found the wrong residuum. "What he ought to have reached as the irreducible basis of all thought, including doubt, was the subject-object relationship."[3] This kind of academic doubt is really only a make-believe and would not have occupied men's

[1] *Mens Creatrix*, pp. 38f.

[2] *Nature, Man and God*, pp. 65f.

[3] Ibid., p. 66. Cf. Paul Tillich, *Systematic Theology*, I (Chicago: The University of Chicago Press, 1951), pp. 164, 169ff, for a similar metaphysical analysis by a contemporary theologian.

minds except that it represented a deeper need, the need to fill the vacuum caused by the collapse of the authority of the medieval tradition.

Temple believes that Descartes, having only the initial certainty of thought without any object, had to affirm that the mind knows nothing directly except its own ideas. By restating the Ontological Argument he established the existence of a God who could be trusted not to give his creatures any clear and distinct ideas which were not true. But this argument is circular in a vicious manner, because the Ontological Argument depends for its validity upon the reliability of clear and distinct ideas which are established only by means of it. Even if the argument were valid, there would be no reason for accepting its conclusion as an apprehension of reality. Having confined himself to self-consciousness as the only immediate datum, Descartes has no right to believe in the existence of anything else at all except his self and its states. "Solipsism is the only logical issue of his initial procedure."[1] However, Descartes used this means to avoid solipsism and to establish the reality of the world as well as of his mind and God.

On the Continent the implications of the rationalist element in Descartes' position were worked out, namely, the insistence that clear and distinct ideas give secure knowledge, so that reality is regarded as subject to the laws of thought. Spinoza treated Descartes' substances, mind and world, as attributes of the one substance, God. The fact that thought and extension were attributes of the one substance guaranteed a correspondence between them, but it becomes impossible to explain how error is possible and how the one substance is affected by such a failure of correspondence between its two attributes. Temple asserts that the religious passion of the Fifth Book of Spinoza's *Ethics* cannot be reconciled with the elementary terms used to describe the one substance, which terms were necessitated by the Cartesian preference for clear

---

[1] *Nature, Man and God*, p. 68.

and distinct ideas. "The essential incoherence of Spinoza is one of the first warning signs of the false lead given to 'modern thought' by its founder."[1] Leibniz dealt dogmatically with the same problem by the theory of a pre-established harmony, not between thought and extension but between isolated monads in which objects occurred as appearances.

In England the Cartesian system was subjected to empirical criticism. Locke held that since the mind gets all its material from sensations, only extension is real, because only extension is measurable and thus capable of producing the necessary clear and distinct ideas. Berkeley continued the criticism and proved that these primary qualities must go the way of the secondary qualities. He thus abolished independent objective existence apart from spiritual entities and left only God and the mind with its ideas. Hume showed that on this basis there was no ground for believing in either God or the mind but only in an unexplained flux of ideas.

With a new method Kant attempted the reconciliation of these two traditions which traced their origin to Descartes. He began with the tradition which followed the Cartesian way of clear and distinct ideas and with the notion of discrete sensations which is the result of the Cartesian dichotomy of mind and extension. He transferred Hume's principles of association from the impressions received to the mind which receives them. According to Kant the mind organizes its discrete sensations by means of the forms and categories. But these sensations are produced by Things-in-Themselves which are unknowable. Knowledge therefore is of phenomena only.

Kant failed because "he never discarded the fatal Cartesian hypothesis that the mind deals directly not with objects known throughout as objects, but with its own ideas which have to be related to the real world by a special act. . . . The real upshot of the argument of [the first] *Critique* is Berkeleyan Idealism

[1] Ibid., p. 69.

with the Thing-in-Itself attached as an illogical appendage."[1] The second and third *Critiques* represent increasing liberation from the Cartesian impasse but only at a sacrifice of consistency with his original doctrine. Kant's Cartesian preference for clear and distinct ideas led him to consider mathematics and physics as the norm of knowledge. If the sciences of biology and history had been as fully developed, the story of modern philosophy might have been quite different.

The English Hegelians with the benefit of the knowledge of these sciences attempted to assert the primary unity which Kant had failed to construct. They emphasized the fact that the distinction between the self and the not-self is made within the given unity of experience. But since they had not completely discarded the Cartesian starting-point, they were led to a position which assumed the epistemological and thus the metaphysical priority of the subject in the subject-object relation of knowledge. Thus, the history of modern philosophy everywhere illustrates "the inherent error of its initial assumption that in knowledge the mind begins with itself and proceeds to the apprehension of the external world by way of construction and inference".[2]

Temple's main contention about modern philosophy is that it has assumed that intellection or cognition is the initial form of apprehension and that other forms of apprehension are evolved from this. From this assumption comes the plausibility of the notion that we begin with mind and its ideas and then proceed by inference to knowledge of the external world. As a result of the progress of science, however, it has become clear that intellectual apprehension is not primary but derivative. Science presented a picture of the world as existing long before the human intellect existed to apprehend it. For a while philosophers tried to solve this difficulty by postulating a divine intelligence as thinking the universe into existence, but this was clearly only an attempt to preserve the priority of

---

[1] *Nature, Man and God*, pp. 70f.　　　[2] Ibid., p. 73.

intellection. Science proceeded to show that intelligence had developed from unconscious organic reaction and instinct, that intellect was a function of organism involved in its interaction with its environment. Philosophy has been mainly concerned with the implications of the fact that the world is intelligible to mind. Recently the split between philosophy and science has been narrowed down by the concern of such philosophers as Bosanquet and Pringle-Pattison with the biological sciences and by the concern of such scientifically-minded men as Eddington and Whitehead with the philosphical problems involved in the results of these sciences. "Return to the concrete richness and bewildering variety and still more bewildering interconnexion of actual experience must be the mode of deliverance from the false scent on which Descartes set the modern mind in its search for truth."[1]

This return has lead to the conclusion that "Apprehension takes place within the world and not the world within apprehension".[2] If the scientific postulate of continuity is accepted in the attempt to explain apprehension on the basis of the scientific view of reality, then either apprehension must be understood in terms of the activity of the ultimate products of the analysis of matter, i.e., electrons, protons, neutrons, etc., or this activity must be understood as embryonic apprehensions. Whitehead adopts the latter hypothesis and develops his theory of apprehension in opposition to that of Descartes, Locke, and Hume. He states that for Hume the primary data are percepts and that emotional feelings are necessarily derived from sensations, while for himself the primary data are "prehensions" which may be non-conscious. He concludes that consciousness presupposes experience and not vice versa.[3]

The scientific study of the world shows that the principle of organism finds illustration long before consciousness appears, and thus it is by the organic principle that we must under-

---

[1] Ibid., p. 80. [2] Ibid., p. 111.

[3] *Process and Reality*, pp. 72, 197, 324; quoted by Temple, *Nature, Man and God*, p. 112.

stand apprehension of the world. Vegetable life exhibits organic adjustment to environment. Self-motion begins to appear in a transitional kind of vegetable-animal. Where there is real self-motion we assume that consciousness to direct such motion exists. Presumably the power of self-motion is accompanied by a differentiation of the organism from its environment which would encourage the development of self-consciousness in the organism. As suggested by Bergson the transition from instinct to intelligence is marked by a change from adjustment *to* environment to the adjustment *of* the environment. The latter activity also is likely to encourage the development of self-consciousness in the organism, but it can no more give birth to self-consciousness than can self-motion.

Temple's view of the development of full human self-conscious apprehension is dependent upon Whitehead's *Process and Reality*. This development begins in the pre-natal stage. The embryo is involved in adjustment to environment, so that the new-born child is already well established in this habit of organic self-adjustment which is rudimentary consciousness. Gradually the two factors in this process of adjustment become distinguished, self and not-self, and the self becomes more unified. Consciousness arises first in its emotional form. Apprehension is primarily by direct mediation of emotional tone and only secondarily by sense. The world of the new-born child consists primarily of himself and his mother in mutual relationship. At the beginning the duality of this relationship is still implicit. It is not yet love or faith or knowledge but the basis of all these. The beginning of consciousness is sympathy, the awareness of feeling in some part of the environment and the feeling evoked in response. From this primal sympathy grows a child's understanding of his mother's understanding of persons and things, and then finally comes his own understanding of this world. On the basis of all this comes the awareness of a distinction between the self as it is and the self as it might be, from which arises the possibility of morality. There also appears the distinction of subject and object in experience and with it the possibility of both science and philosophy. But all these are late developments since cognition itself is a late and specialized form of consciousness.

Thus, knowledge of persons precedes knowledge of things. The unified mind does not argue from the behaviour of some objects to the conclusion that they must be animated by minds similar to itself. It is only through its intercourse with other minds that it attains its own unity.

All the activities and distinctions which the mind elaborates are given in the initial datum of experience and are produced by the analysis of what is at first given as an apparently undifferentiated continuum. The realization of all the richness of experience in science, art, and morality "is not achieved by inference from initial percepts, but rather by the direction of attention to the different elements in the initial datum as practical interest, and later theoretic interest also, may require".[1]

Temple concludes that all theories of perception are fallacious which begin with a *sensum* as the object of immediate apprehension and with which the mind builds up a picture of the world which it then believes itself to apprehend. The initial and permanent fact is the organism in interaction with its environment. If the organism is mental, this interaction involves apprehension and this apprehension is of the real world. *Sensa* are part of the mind's machinery of apprehension. "In cognition the subject-object relation is ultimate, and neither term is in any degree reducible to the other."[2] An idea is not some *tertium quid* mediating between the mind and reality. An idea is a mental apprehension of reality; it is essentially the thinking mind. But because the mind is self-conscious, it can think about itself as thinking and thereby make its own ideas into its objects. "If we begin with the

---

[1] *Nature, Man and God*, p. 128.   [2] Ibid., p. 126.

notion that the mind never has any objects except its own ideas, we can never argue to a world beyond at all."[1]

In his affirmation of realism, however, Temple avoids a naïve realism, the view that apart from knowledge an object is exactly the same as it is for knowledge. The mind may misapprehend reality. Its ideas may be adequate or inadequate; apprehension although genuine may be vague and confused.[2]

This leads directly to the interpretive and critical aspect of apprehension, the contribution of the mind to apprehension. If an apprehension is inadequate, knowledge of the reality apprehended requires a reflective and critical process which goes beyond what is given in perception. However, it does not depart from the perception but rather interprets what it truly is. All apprehension contains this element of interpretation from the beginning. It is impossible for a rational being to apprehend anything without rationalizing it in the process. If we had a sensation which was only a sensation and nothing more, we would be unaware of it. The material of thought is always a sensation which has been named or attached to a universal. There is no such thing as the initial grasp of mere particulars apart from all generalization. We never experience a mere "this" without its also being a "such". It is always already this instance of such and such a thing, *tode toionde*. Conversely, it is also impossible to hold a universal or concept in thought without some percept or image. All thought must have some real object or equivalent of a real object.[3]

It is on the basis of this organic and critical realism that Temple bases his views of knowledge or truth. All mental activity begins as a means of satisfying the need or appetition

---

[1] *Mens Creatrix*, p. 51. For Temple's statement of his realistic epistemology, see *The Faith and Modern Thought*, p. xi; *Mens Creatrix*, pp. 50f; *Nature, Man and God*, pp. 109–28, 139, 146f, 490.

[2] *Mens Creatrix*, p. 51; *Nature, Man and God*, pp. 126, 146.

[3] *Mens Creatrix*, pp. 19n, 36f, 54; *Christ the Truth*, pp. 45f; *Nature, Man and God*, pp. 126, 146f.

of the organism. Some elements in the environment are perceived as having meaning for the organism as objects of desire or affection. If such an element is an object of desire, it is its generic quality which causes the selective attention of the organism to be directed toward it. In the later forms of development of consciousness this desire may become the will to know, the impulse which is the basis of science. At this level vestiges of its origin in desire will be seen in the choice of major premises or the area of concentration. As the original desire was concerned with generalities, the capacity for satisfying desires, so the scientific impulse is also concerned with generalities, the universal which is abstracted from the particulars. Mind fixes its attention on general qualities of objects, detaches them in thought from the objects, and thus forms concepts or "free ideas" which are the instruments of scientific thought.

In the scientific enterprise there is a growing apprehension of reality which illustrates the contention that there is a correlation between mind and reality.[1] This discovery of a kinship of mind and reality invests knowledge with a value of its own apart from any utilitarian value.[2] This leads to the search for knowledge for its own sake, to the attitude that true knowledge is not merely a means of satisfaction but something august which can claim man's allegiance and service.

Temple concludes that this scientific truth is "that ideal intellectual construction which would reveal the principles governing the real world in their complete nexus, . . . that system of notions which would give perfect intellectual satisfaction".[3] This scientific truth is a universal and all-pervasive aspect of the real world, and nothing can claim exemption from the criticism and analysis of the scientific intellect. However, scientific truth is not reality but only one element in reality which is a complex including many other elements.

---

[1] See Chapter 3.   [2] See Chapter 6.
[3] *Mens Creatrix*, p. 50.

Its type is mathematics and it is marked by absolute cogency, timelessness, and abstractness, which are at once its strengths and weaknesses.

If an element in the environment of an organism is an object of affection, it is the individuality of the object which is attended to, and this individuality is a union of universal and particular. The relation of affection is just as much a relation of knowledge as is that of desire. This knowledge is never final but always growing in depth rather than in extension. It is impossible to give this kind of knowledge scientific expression; it can be expressed only through art by the use of imagination.[1]

---

[1] *Mens Creatrix*, pp. 9f, 33ff, 50, 68, 89; *Nature, Man and God*, pp. 138–53, 201f. The question of whether Temple's epistemology is consistently realistic will be discussed in Chapter 8.

6

VALUE

TEMPLE's theory of value proceeds directly from his realistic epistemology and more specifically from his organic view of the relation of mind to its environment. The basic fact with reference to value is the mind in organic relation to and interaction with its environment.[1] The essential condition of value is the correspondence between mind and its environment. This is one form of Temple's basic metaphysical presupposition that the universe is a rational unity.[2]

Temple describes this correspondence variously as a kinship, an at-homeness, a correlation, mind finding itself, its own kin, what is akin to itself, its own nature, its own characteristics, its own principle, the principles of its own nature, or the counterpart of the principles of its activities, in its object. Mind's discovery of this kinship is

> an experience which has two aspects: first, that it finds the counterpart of the principle of its own activities as for example the mathematical properties of mechanical combinations of forces or of aesthetic proportions; secondly, that with this discovery goes a feeling of being at home with the object, not lost or bewildered in presence of it.[3]

Temple's definition of value varies slightly in his major works. In *Christ the Truth* he states that value is not a relation of subject and object but "a unitary system of experience"

[1] *Mens Creatrix*, p. 165; *Nature, Man and God*, pp. 128f, 138–41, 218; *Christianity in Thought and Practice*, p. 25.

[2] See Chapter 3.

[3] *Nature, Man and God*, p. 165; cf. pp. 129ff, 148ff, 152ff, 164, 166ff, 190, 193, 208, 218f, 247ff; *Christ the Truth*, pp. 29, 39; *Christianity in Thought and Practice*, p. 26.

which involves such a relation.[1] In the Gifford Lectures value
is a relation. It is the correlation of reality with knowledge or
appreciation.[2] This seems to be Temple's final formulation,
and in it he attempts to balance the subjective and objective
factors. He argues against the view that it is impossible to
attribute value to reality in itself, that value is found only in
states of consciousness. He also argues against the view of
Alexander that beauty involves "satisfactoriness in the
object". This seems to him to make the value too subjective
and to involve the adaptation of the object to the subject,
whereas the reverse seems to be true of the experience of
value. He urges that value is objective, that value is in the
object, not in the appreciating mind. The mind discovers the
value in the object rather than creating it. It is the object
apprehended and not the apprehension which is of value. "To
doubt the objectivity of Value is to adopt what has been
called Scepticism of the Instrument in so extreme a form as to
make all intellectual effort futile."[3]

But if value is objectively real, it is also subjectively conditioned. This becomes clear in Temple's disagreement with
G. E. Moore over the value of an unapprehended beautiful
world. Moore holds that it would be desirable that the maximum amount of beauty should exist even though no mind,
divine, angelic, or human, should appreciate it.[4] Temple
claims that he can attach no meaning to this statement. Value
consists of an interaction or correlation of mind and environment, of subject and object. Apart from conscious apprehension and appreciation value is either non-existent or exists
only potentially. In one of his earlier works he states that the
existence of value begins with appreciation, and that apart

---

[1] P. 39.

[2] *Nature, Man and God*, pp. 149, 165.

[3] Ibid., p. 215; cf. pp. 152, 154f, 163ff, 211; *Mens Creatrix*, p. 84;
Christ the Truth, p. 21; *Christianity in Thought and Practice*, pp. 26, 28.

[4] *Principia Ethica*, pp. 83–5; referred to, *Mens Creatrix*, p. 84, *Christ the
Truth*, p. 21; *Christianity in Thought and Practice*, p. 26.

from consciousness, value is non-existent.[1] In his later works, however, he uses the potentiality-actuality distinction.

> Value is only actual in the various things that are valuable; and it is only *fully* actual . . . so far as it is appreciated by some conscious being.
>
> . . . .
>
> Value is dormant or potential until appreciation awakes it to energy and actuality.
>
> Appreciation brings to actuality a quality of the object which previously belonged to it *really*, but potentially and not actually —*ontos* but *dunamei* not *energeia*.
>
> There would be no *effective* good in the existence of the beautiful object, and therefore no beauty conceived as a value, unless it were apprehended.[2]

The subjective-objective character of value raises the question of the relation of value to existence, the question of the relation of fact and value, which Temple felt to be the main philosophical problem of his day. He denies Unamuno's radical dualism between facts and values. He criticizes Pringle-Pattison for making values appendices adjectival to the facts of an existing universe.[3] He claims that philosophy has often held values to be states of consciousness or external attributes of things, because it has tended to take the natural sciences as the normative subject matter of its inquiry. Philosophers have generally made existence their substantive notion while value has become adjectival. Plato's main propaedeutic study for apprehending the Idea of the Good is geometry rather than ethics or politics. Although Aquinas identifies good with being, he treats being as prior and defines substance as that which exists of itself. Philosophy has been slow to accept the human

[1] *Mens Creatrix*, p. 84.

[2] *Christ the Truth*, pp. 18, 21; *Nature, Man and God*, pp. 211f; *Christianity in Thought and Practice*, p. 26; italics added. Cf. *The Nature of Personality*, p. 71; *Christ the Truth*, p. 22; *Nature, Man and God*, pp. 153f; *Christianity in Thought and Practice*, p. 28.

[3] "Some Implications of Theism", pp. 415f; *Christ the Truth*, pp. 11ff, 24.

activities of moral conduct and art as the normative subject matter, perhaps because they involve emotional and volitional elements which cannot be dealt with as precisely as the results of the natural sciences. Since human activities are directed toward values, any philosophy which takes the former seriously must have an integral place for values.[1]

Temple believes that a philosopher in order to interpret the world process must decide whether his interpretation will begin with the lowest or with the highest categories. The philosophy inspired by physical science is guided by the maxim that any event or datum must be accounted for by the lowest adequate category, usually matter, atoms, or their smallest particles. In such a scheme the appearance of mind and value is a discontinuity which can be explained only by theories treating them as epiphenomena which produce no modification in the process. Since such theories do not do justice to the facts, Temple concludes:

> If we begin with mindless and valueless fact we cannot give any place in our scheme to Mind or Value without breaking up the unity of the scheme itself. The very activity which makes science possible remains unaccounted for in the theory of the world which men have constructed in the activity of science.[2]

It would, however, be a repetition of the Cartesian blunder to begin with mind and to try to explain matter in terms of it. We must start with the given totality of experience of the process in which mind and matter are given elements. This is, in fact, the picture which modern science gives of the world process. In this totality mind is always aware of value or disvalue in its environment. In actual experience fact and value are given together. However, although fact or existence is not of itself in principle able to give rise to value, value in principle can give rise to fact. This is certainly the case in human production, since all human activity is value-oriented. When this example is extended to include all existence,

---

[1] *Christ the Truth*, pp. 13–15.   [2] *Nature, Man and God*, p. 216.

the result is the theistic hypothesis, namely, that all existence is dependent upon the purposive, value-oriented action of a supreme mind. The theistic hypothesis involves the logical priority of value to existence. Objects come into existence because they are good or means to good.[1]

Temple proceeds to discuss the ontological status of value, its relation to substance. He claims that the identity of substance with value follows from the theistic hypothesis. The universe receives its existence from the Creative Will. But the correlative of will is good or value; will is always aimed at the realization of value. Therefore, the most fundamental element, the constitutive principle of every existent, is its value. The primary ground of existence is the Creative Will, and value, since it is the object of the Creative Will, is the secondary ground of existence. Thus, although value is logically prior to existence, it does not include existence and must receive existence to be a part of reality. But nothing receives existence except as a realization of value or as a means to value.

Thus, Temple would define substance as value plus existence. But if substance is distinguished from accidents, then substance is identical with value. In a philosophy which adopts value as its main substantive notion, ethics, politics, and aesthetics will be more normative than mathematics and the natural sciences. Such a philosophy would remove the tension between value and existence which is widespread in contemporary philosophy. It would hold the objective and the subjective together at the very point at which the tension between them has appeared, namely, in human consciousness. It is here that the clear distinction between subject and object appears, and it is here that the conscious appreciation of value appears wherein subject and object are united. Also, it is man

[1] Ibid., pp. 207f, 213–20; cf. *The Nature of Personality*, p. xxvii; *Mens Creatrix*, pp. 88f; "Some Implications of Theism", p. 428; *Christ the Truth*, p. 11; *Christianity in Thought and Practice*, p. 25; *Religious Experience*, p. 79. For a further elaboration of this point, see Chapter 11.

who first raises the question of the explanation of the world, and it is in man's appreciation of value that the answer appears. The solution of the problem of existence is found in the experience of what is good.

> Everything except the Creative Will exists to be the expression of that Will, the actualization of its values, and the communication of those values to spirits created for the special value actualized through fellowship in creation and appreciation of values.[1]

Closely connected with Temple's emphasis on the objectivity of value is his affirmation that value is irreducible and unanalysable and that value judgements are intuitive, ultimate, and final. Value is an irreducible aspect or function of reality. The terms which express it cannot be analysed or translated into the terms of any other category or expressed in the terms of any particular science. Appreciation of the meaning of such terms is independent of argument. Thus, it is impossible to argue *a priori* to the goodness of anything in particular. It follows that we can appreciate value or goodness only by direct experience. In the realm of moral value, therefore, the "moral sense" school of philosophy is right. The intention of the term "good" may be known *a priori*, but its extension only by experience. Thus, Plato in order to commend justice merely exhibited it in the life of the individual and the state. Furthermore, there can be no argument about intrinsic (as distinguished from instrumental) value; there is approval or there is not.

Taste, appreciation, and sensitivity may be trained, but the method of training is always submission to authority. If an individual's judgement continues to differ from that of the expert or the general consensus, nothing more can be done. All value judgements are intuitive, ultimate, and final. Although the faculties of intuition may be trained, there is no

---

[1] *Christ the Truth*, p. 19; cf. pp. 16–19, 22f, 25; "Some Implications of Theism", pp. 420ff, 427f; *Religious Experience*, pp. 81ff.

other appeal. Temple quotes F. H. Bradley on this point: "Our sense of value, and in the end for every man his own sense of value, is ultimate and final. And, since there is no court of appeal, it is idle to inquire if this sense is fallible."[1]

This position would seem to lead to a chaos of individualism in the realm of value, but Temple avoids this by associating his value theory with his theory of society. Since all values cannot be realized in one person, the society of persons is necessary for the full actualization of all the values in the world. Thus, each person as a unique and irreplaceable member of society will have certain values which he should realize. In order to fulfill his particular function in society, a person must have a certain character. And since value judgements depend upon character, the place which a person is called to hold in the structure of society will determine those particular values he is called upon to realize in his life. Thus, finite persons contribute to the commonwealth of value which is suggested as the ultimate fulfilment by the theistic hypothesis.[2]

Temple believes that the value of past events is not unalterable. The value of any event is not fixed until the series of which it is a member is complete. In some of his works Temple means by this that the value of an experience lasting through a period of time depends on its tendency and conclusion and not upon the stages in isolation. In other works he means that an event which was considered evil may turn out to be an integral and necessary element in a larger good, although the event does not cease to be evil. It is not clear that either case is a real change of value. The change appears in the relation of the event to its total context which unfolds

---

[1] *Mind*, N.S. LXVI (April 1908), p. 230, and *Essays on Truth and Reality*, p. 132; quoted, *The Nature of Personality*, pp. 72; *The Kingdom of God*, p. 44; *Mens Creatrix*, p. 180; *Nature, Man and God*, p. 53; see also *The Nature of Personality*, pp. 71, 75; *The Kingdom of God*, p. 43; *Plato and Christianity*, pp. 38f, 72; *Mens Creatrix*, pp. 178f, 187, 199; *Christ the Truth*, p. 29; *Christian Faith and Life*, p. 46; *Nature, Man and God*, p. 175.

[2] *The Nature of Personality*, pp. 72f; *The Kingdom of God*, pp. 44–7; *Mens Creatrix*, pp. 83–5, 179–81; *Nature, Man and God*, lecture xvi,

in time. Although an event may have been merely bad, now it may be an integral element in good, not simply outweighed by later good. This becomes an important factor in Temple's attempt to deal with the problem of evil.[1] Temple summarizes:

> The future does not merely disclose in the past something which was always there, but causes the past, while retaining its own nature, actually to be, in its organic union with its consequence, something which in isolation it neither is nor was.[2]

This is one case of Temple's general principle that totality is the distinguishing feature of value, the very form of value. All valuable objects are marked by this totality or comprehensive unity. "Science seeks a totality of perpetually wider extension; Art seeks a totality of perfected inner unity; Goodness is the achievement of inner unity in the individual and extended unity in the society—totality in both."[3] The standard of the mind in the search for truth is totality, the embrace of all relevant reality in a comprehensive unity. The standard of the mind in the search for beauty and goodness is the same totality, which is one of the forms of Temple's basic metaphysical presupposition.[4]

A final aspect of the nature of value is its relation to the satisfaction or pleasure which accompanies its apprehension and appreciation. There are two problems here: the relation of value to this satisfaction and the value of the satisfaction itself. In the first place, it is clear that for Temple intellectual, aesthetic, and moral value does not reside in the apprehension or appreciation but in the object, although this value is actualized only by means of the apprehension or appreciation. In the appreciation of value, however, subjective satisfaction or pleasure has a necessary place. Value is recognized by the

---

[1] See Chapter 7.

[2] *Nature, Man and God*, p. 210; cf. pp. 177, 209, 212; *The Nature of Personality*, pp. 67ff; *Mens Creatrix*, pp. 172ff; *Christ the Truth*, p. 40.

[3] *Christ the Truth*, p. 39.

[4] Ibid., pp. 39f; *Nature, Man and God*, pp. 166f.

sense of satisfaction felt when mind finds what is akin to itself
in its object. Mind admires the object in which it finds value,
but it also enjoys the apprehension. Temple believes that this
satisfaction, enjoyment, or pleasure associated with the appreciation of value is itself good and valuable, and that the value
thus experienced is the feeling, but he is not clear on the
relation of this value to the triad of intellectual, aesthetic, and
moral value. Pleasure is not the highest value, but is derivative
and secondary and finds only a subordinate place in a perfect
life. Although Temple holds that satisfaction, pleasure, and
enjoyment, whether or not associated with the higher values,
are real values, it is not clear how they fall under the general
definition of value as the discovery by mind of what is akin to
itself in its object.[1]

Temple begins his discussion of the forms of value with an
analysis of the traditional triad of absolute values, truth,
beauty, and goodness, as distinguished from relative values,
such as pleasure. In *Christ the Truth* this triad is considered to
be three forms of the one absolute value, love, which uses each
of the three as a channel to reveal and communicate itself.
These values or forms of value are inherent, i.e., good in
themselves, and absolute, i.e., independent of comparison and
consequences. They may, however, become rivals through
force of circumstance, such as insufficient time. In cases of
conflict goodness has a priority over the other two, because
it is the distinctively human type of value. This means that in
goodness human creation predominates, while in truth and
beauty, appreciation predominates. Also, it is possible to
pursue truth and beauty selfishly, but this is not possible in
the case of goodness. Furthermore, since value is mind's discovery of what is akin to itself in its object, the highest value
will be in mind's relation to other minds. Thus, moral goodness is the highest value, and its perfection is love.

[1] *Christ the Truth*, pp. 29ff, 38f; *Nature, Man and God*, pp. 152ff, 165, 412;
Christianity in Thought and Practice, p. 26.

In the Gifford Lectures Temple modifies his analysis and concludes that truth and beauty are relative and not absolute. It is not always good that everyone should be in possession of all possible truth or be confronted by all possible beauty. The result is that truth and beauty are good *ceteris paribus*. (But is this not also true of pleasure and other relative values?) This absoluteness of goodness is maintained on the basis that no circumstances could ever arise in which it would be better that a man were not as good as he is. However, it would seem that appreciation of moral value might come under the same strictures as appreciation of aesthetic value. If it could be the case that the contemplation of a consummate work of art might have a demoralizing effect upon those who are immature in aesthetic appreciation, the same might be the case in the contemplation of an action of the highest moral value, although it would not be the case in the carrying out of such an action. If it is argued that at least the creation of moral value is absolute, is not this also true of the creation of aesthetic value? Temple does not give a satisfactory answer to these questions.[1]

Temple outlines his interpretation of the forms of value as different activities in which mind discovers itself or its own principles in its object.

> When Mind makes this discovery in the activity of contemplation, the form of Value actualized is Beauty. When Mind makes this discovery in the activity of analysis and synthesis, the form of value actualized is Truth. When Mind makes this discovery in the activity of personal relationship, the form of value actualized is Goodness.[2]

Temple is concerned to elaborate his views on the theory of value not only because it is a live philosophical problem, but also because he believes that it suggests theism as a final philosophical synthesis and because it supplies a necessary

---

[1] *Christ the Truth*, pp. 29–38; *Nature, Man and God*, pp. 135–8, 167f.
[2] *Nature, Man and God*, p. 164.

step in his argument for theism. For example, he believes that there would be an exceeding value in the unity of all possible values in the universe. This suggests the possibility of an infinite mind in which all possible values are actualized. Another possibility is that since values are objective, we should read them back into the ultimate ground of the system of reality. Furthermore, since value is the explanation of fact in the case of human production, and since a final explanation of the universe could only be in terms of purpose or will, which alone combine efficient and final causation, there is the possibility that an infinite mind which appreciates all the possible values of the world may also be a creative will which has produced the universe for the sake of its value. Thus, God is not the sum of all possible values, the Idea of the Good, as Plato first called the ultimate principle, but he is the creative will actualizing all possible values eternally, or the "royal mind of Zeus", as Plato later described him more adequately.

Temple would agree, however, that it is not absolutely necessary that there should be an explanation of the universe. If any philosophical synthesis is internally coherent, nothing further can be demanded logically. It is an advantage if any theory can explain the existence of the universe, but it is not fatal to a theory if it should fail in this. It may be that there is no such explanation or that it is inaccessible to the human mind. Such a universe would have intellectual value, but it would have no moral value. But if rationality manifests itself in the apprehension of ultimate value wherein all other values cohere with each other and with existence, then such a universe would not be rational. Thus, if rationality be so defined, there would have to be a choice between a theory which offered such an explanation and complete scepticism, since scepticism is the only alternative to the postulation of a rational universe. This gives weight to such a theory as the one suggested by Temple's theory of value which is described above.

From this Temple concludes that every apprehension of value is in principle a religious experience and an inchoate apprehension of God. The experience of truth and beauty is an unambiguous affirmation of a wholly other and transcendent mind apprehended by reason of its immanence in the world. In the pursuit of beauty, truth, and goodness we are entering into fellowship with a mind and spirit itself characterized by these three in the highest degree.[1]

Besides this suggestive use of his value theory, there is Temple's use of it in the dialectical argument for theism in the Gifford Lectures. Value is that relationship or kinship between mind and the world process which is the basis of the first dialectical transition: from the picture of the world offered by science through the appearance of mind to immanent theism. If mind is produced in the world process, then because of the nature of mind in relation to process, this process must be grounded in mind or find its explanation in terms of mind. Furthermore, value is always the object of purpose or will in mind, and purpose or will is a self-explanatory principle which offers a possible explanation of the existence of the world.

Value also plays a part in the second dialectical transition: from immanent theism through the nature of personality to transcendent theism. The experience of value is intelligible only if it involves a relation to personal spirit, a reverence which can only be claimed by that which is personal and transcendent in relation to process. Finally, Temple describes the fulfilment of the universe under the ordering of the divine will in terms of a commonwealth of value.[2]

---

[1] *Mens Creatrix*, pp. 88f; "Some Implications of Theism", pp. 427f; *Christ the Truth*, pp. 7–11, 16, 19, 40–3, 47f, 114; *Nature, Man and God*, pp. 156f, 161, 219f, 249–55, 282; *Christianity in Thought and Practice*, pp. 28ff, 72ff; *Religious Experience*, p. 80.

[2] *Nature, Man and God*, lectures vi–viii, x, xvi. See Part II.

7

NEGATIVE VALUE:
THE PROBLEM OF EVIL

In a philosophy of religion such as Temple's in which the concept of value plays a central rôle the existence of negative value or evil becomes a serious problem. If in the end the explanation of everything is to be found in the good purpose of an eternal will, the problem is, what is the good of evil? or, why does a good God either create or permit evil?[1]

Temple relates his theory of evil to his value theory only in the Gifford Lectures. In his earlier works and when he is not relating it to his value theory, evil is analysed into three forms: intellectual, emotional, and moral: error, pain or suffering, and sin.[2] In the Gifford Lectures where he relates it directly to his value theory, evil is defined as negative value and is analysed into three forms: ignorance, error, or falsity; ugliness; and baseness, moral evil, or sin. Negative value is the situation in which mind finds nothing akin to itself in its object or finds something which is akin but hostile, antagonistic, or alien.

> When Mind in its aesthetic activity of contemplation finds what is strange and alien, that is the experience of Ugliness. When Mind in its scientific activity of analysis and synthesis finds itself bewildered and baffled by its environment, or when it acquiesces in an apparent recognition of its own principle in that environment, to which other facts than those under observation are recalcitrant, that is the experience of Ignorance or Error. When Mind in its ethical activity of determining personal

[1] *Mens Creatrix*, p. 262.
[2] *The Faith and Modern Thought*, p. 121; *Mens Creatrix*, p. 273; *Nature, Man and God*, p. 509.

relationships either fails to find its counterpart, or finds it as something akin, indeed, but hostile, that is the experience of Moral Evil.[1]

Temple does not explain how suffering or emotional evil fits into this latter scheme. Its place seems to be taken by ugliness, but there is no discussion of the possible correlation of these two forms of evil. This is not a later development of his thought, because he returns to the former scheme later in the Gifford Lectures.[2] There seems to be nothing in common between suffering and the other forms of evil as far as Temple's value theory is concerned.[3] Furthermore, neither scheme includes the tragic form of evil, the defect or conflict within the good, with which Temple deals at some length in *Mens Creatrix*.

In *Mens Creatrix* Temple shows how tragedy casts light on the problem of evil. Evil is a positive force which takes advantage of a defect in good and enhances the good. Evil is also the conflict of good with itself, the defect within good which makes it serve evil at a critical moment. Evil is finally purged only through a partial destruction of good. Tragedy reveals the world as terrible but as nobler than it would be without evil. In tragedy, however, the solution of the problem of evil is felt but not understood. Tragedy indicates that the problem is soluble, but the intellect is still perplexed.[4]

Although Temple is nearer to idealism in his early period, in *Mens Creatrix* he rejects the idealist solution of the problem of evil as presented by Bradley. Bradley suggests that ultimate reality is super-moral, that any discord disappears if the harmony is made wide enough, and that because ultimate reality is a unity, every element of the universe must be absolutely good.[5] Temple suggests that this doctrine of the illusory

---

[1] *Nature, Man and God*, p. 357; cf. pp. 164, 218.   [2] Ibid., p. 509.
[3] Cf. Tremenheere, review of *Nature, Man and God*, *Theology*, XXXI (November 1935), p. 285.
[4] *Mens Creatrix*, pp. 144f, 150ff, 261.
[5] Temple refers here to *Appearance and Reality*, pp. 202, 412.

character of evil also proclaims that evil is irredeemable. The problem of evil is solved not by the overcoming of evil but by the transcending of the distinction between good and evil. Temple believes this to be not only pessimistic but also irrational. If value is the highest category and the presupposition of knowledge in that the will to know is grounded in value, then an absolutism which transcends value is self-contradictory.[1]

Temple also rejects the suggestion that the problem of evil is solved by calling evil a negativity, an absence of something, a privation, or non-being. Nor can evil be regarded as the necessary consequence of the existence of finite spirits. Another possibility which he rejects is the denial of divine omnipotence. The category of quantity cannot be applied to the power of the creator who is the self-explanatory ground of the existence of the universe. "If Goodness is the only ground of existence, the distinction of Goodness and Power in God is only 'provisionally' justifiable."[2]

Thus, the problem is to show that evil is a necessary means to the greatest good that the nature of good itself makes possible. One of the most conspicuous forms of good is victory over evil and this requires the existence of the evil. Temple maintains that evil overcome by good is often justified, and consequently the ultimate solution of the problem is to be found in action rather than in thought. He admits that this requires an infinite time series. To the objection that such a series involves an indeterminism, he replies that the concept of a self-determined process with no beginning is not contradictory. To the objection that this involves a denial of the meaning of progress since there can be no goal, he replies that ethical progress does not necessarily require a goal. "Evil, in the general sense of opposition to Good, may never perish; but every special form of evil perishes and the Progress is not illusory but real."[3] A. E. Taylor in commenting on this

---

[1] *Mens Creatrix*, pp. 264f; *The Kingdom of God*, p. 107.
[2] *Mens Creatrix*, p. 267.   [3] Ibid., p. 273

discussion points out that there are infinite mathematical series which have first and last terms and that Temple therefore need not insist on the absence of such terms in order to affirm infinite progress.[1]

Temple defines error as unwarrantable synthesis, a disregard of the differences between things. It is part of the experimental character of life. Intellectual life derives much of its stimulus from the element of adventure in generalizations. "Error is an element in the very goodness of the search for truth."[2] To Joachim's objection that the existence of error contradicts the reality of an omniscient God, Temple replies that divine omniscience is not all-inclusive experience and need not be understood to suffer the errors that it knows to be the condition of finite minds.[3]

Suffering is justified when its courageous endurance is inspired by love, when it is met by real sympathy, when it is gladly endured for a worthy cause, and when it perfects love. The combination of suffering with these things is better than the absence of all. But this justification is only in principle and requires the presence of these conditions in order to be actualized.[4]

One of the most difficult aspects of evil for Temple is the tragic fact, the conflict of the good with itself and the inherent defects in certain types of goodness. The great virtues involve an element of moral risk, and they lead to destruction when confronted with certain evils. Temple sees this as part of the maladjustment of the world which is necessary if there is to be effort and progress in morality. He suggests that tragedy may be justified in part by the sympathy it produces.[5]

The essence of sin is self-will, the ignoring or repudiation of

---

[1] Review of *Mens Creatrix*, *Mind*, N.S. XXVII (April 1918), p. 231.

[2] *Mens Creatrix*, p. 275.

[3] Ibid., pp. 273–8; cf. *The Nature of Personality*, pp. 84f.

[4] *The Faith and Modern Thought*, pp. 122f, "The Divinity of Christ", *Foundations*, p. 220; *Mens Creatrix*, pp. 278–82; *Nature, Man and God*, pp. 502, 509f.

[5] *Mens Creatrix*, pp. 282ff.

the claims of other spirits, human and divine. The justification of self-will is that love is perfected in the self-surrender which overcomes self-will. "In fact a sinful world redeemed by the agony of Love's complete self-sacrifice is a better world, by the only standards of excellence we have, than a world that had never sinned."[1] To the objection that therefore we should continue in sin that grace and love might abound, Temple replies that it is psychologically impossible at the same time both to will that grace and love should abound and to continue in sin. The mode of the victory of love over sin is to elicit love, to call out the response of love by the manifestation of it in its irresistible power.[2]

In *Christ the Truth* Temple points out that the statement of the problem of evil and its solution in *Mens Creatrix* is presented in terms of general philosophy without regard to the Christian revelation. Evil may be justified by the fact that it affords the occasion for a higher form of good than would be possible without it. This is identical with the solution given by Bosanquet whom Temple quotes approvingly.[3] Temple proceeds in *Christ the Truth* and in other works to present as the actual justification of evil the Christian doctrine of the atonement along Abelardian lines. God the creator has manifested his love in such a way that sin is being overcome and transformed into love.[4]

It is only in his later works that Temple addresses himself to the problem of the origin of sin. Although there is one suggestion in an earlier work that sin is at least in part attributable to "our evolutionary descent from non-human

---

[1] Ibid., p. 286.

[2] Ibid., pp. 284–92; cf. *The Faith and Modern Thought*, pp. 124f; "The Divinity of Christ", pp. 220f; *Christ the Truth*, p. 256.

[3] *The Principle of Individuality and Value*, pp. 243–54, quoted or referred to by Temple, *Mens Creatrix*, p. 292; *Christ the Truth*, pp. 303, 325; *Nature, Man and God*, pp. 508f.

[4] *Christ the Truth*, pp. 303, 311f, 322–6; cf. *The Faith and Modern Thought*, 134ff; "The Divinity of Christ", p. 221; *Mens Creatrix*, p. 292; *Nature, Man and God*, pp. 376, 397, 400, 519f; *The Centrality of Christ*, p. 76.

ancestors",[1] in his later works Temple rejects any evolutionary account of the origin of moral evil. The theory that the source of sin is in the survival of animal impulses disregards the fact that the seat of trouble is the will or the spirit, not the appetites. The theory of N. P. Williams that the source of sin is a defect of the gregarious instinct disregards the fact that the strengthening of this instinct can produce groups and movements which can be terribly destructive.[2]

The theory of the origin of sin which Temple elaborates is based on his value theory and the application of a spatial metaphor to the nature of the self. Man is a centre of the appreciation of value, and he is governed by what appears to him to be good. Because he is finite, his apparent good is highly likely to be different from the true good. This is not absolutely necessary, but it is too probable not to happen. Thus, self-consciousness becomes self-centredness and self-assertion. This self-assertion is magnified by imagination and the reciprocity of social influence to produce the moral evil which is apparent in the world. Progress in overcoming self-centredness is possible through the appreciation of value, but this can only be partial. A complete deliverance from sin would involve a sharp break, a conversion, so that the self would be uprooted from its centre in itself and resystematized around God as its centre. This can be accomplished only through a personal manifestation of God's love in an act of sheer self-sacrifice which would win the submission of the self. "When love by its own self-sacrifice has converted self-centredness into love, there is an excellence, alike in the process and in the result, so great as to justify the self-centredness and all the welter of evil flowing from it."[3]

---

[1] *The Nature of Personality*, p. 38.

[2] *Nature, Man and God*, pp. 369f; *The Centrality of Christ*, pp. 62f.

[3] *Nature, Man and God*, pp. 510f; cf. *Christ the Truth*, pp. 256, 323; *Nature, Man and God*, lectures xiv, xv, xx; *The Centrality of Christ*, ch. iii; *Christianity and Social Order*, pp. 37f. The material in the Gifford Lectures will be analysed and criticized in detail in Chapters 13 and 14.

8

MIND

ONE of the basic categories in Temple's philosophy of religion is mind. This category plays a large part in Temple's views on the structure of reality, epistemology, and value, as has been indicated in the preceding chapters. It also supplies the keystone in the first dialectical transition in the argument for theism in the Gifford Lectures. The purpose of this chapter is to bring together the various aspects of Temple's thought on this subject and to examine the coherence of his view of mind. Although nurtured in idealism, Temple claims to criticize this tradition radically and to affirm a realist position. After a consideration of his interpretation of mind, we will be in a position to assess his claim to be called a realist.

Because of his basic metaphysical presupposition that reality is a rational unity, Temple affirms that mind is integrally related to reality, that the principles of activity of mind are true of the real world, and that there is a kinship or correlation between mind and the world. According to his analysis of the structure of reality, mind is a level or grade of reality which is dependent on those levels below it (matter and life) and in which they are fulfilled in so far as they are controlled or indwelt by mind. Similarly, mind is the necessary basis of that level above it (spirit) and is fulfilled only in so far as it is controlled or indwelt by spirit. Mind is a mode of action and reaction involving a capacity for calculation of means to ends presented as valuable.

In his discussions of epistemology Temple concludes that the activities of mind are grounded in the relation of the organism to its environment, and that in the activity of cognition the subject-object relation is ultimate and neither term is in any degree reducible to the other. The scientific and philosophical concern for universals has its origin in the desire of the organism for a generic quality of the object. In its highest form this becomes the capacity of the mind to form free ideas, the ability to abstract universals from particulars. Finally, Temple holds that the essential condition of value is the correspondence between mind and its environment, one form of the metaphysical presupposition mentioned above. Value, although objectively real in the object, is subjectively conditioned and is actualized by the appreciating mind.

All through his major works there is some confusion in Temple's use of the category of mind.[1] In *Mens Creatrix* he uses the terms "mind" and "Mind" in several ways. The term "mind" is used to refer to the human mind as a class,[2] to the individual finite human mind as a particular (singular and plural),[3] and to the infinite mind of God.[4] The term "Mind" also is used to refer to the human mind as a class,[5] to the individual finite human mind as a particular (singular and plural),[6] and to the infinite mind of God.[7] But the term "Mind" is also used in a generic sense which is broader than the human mind as a class and seems to refer to mind as a principle or mode of activity.[8] This seems to be the only distinction between the uses of these two terms.

In *Christ the Truth* the usage is more uniform, and it is stated that "Mind" and the other grades of reality may be understood either "as various entities or as different modes

[1] In the following paragraphs I am indebted to E. G. Harris for some suggestions made in his unpublished master's thesis at Union Theological Seminary, New York, "Some Basic Notions in the Philosophy of Religion of William Temple, Archbishop of Canterbury" (1945).

[2] *Mens Creatrix*, pp. 36, 50f, 84, 258.

[3] Ibid., pp. 82, 88, 126.

[4] Ibid., p. 82.

[5] Ibid., pp. 4, 23, 29, 82, 88ff, 126, 258.

[6] Ibid., pp. 23, 85, 90, 159f.

[7] Ibid., pp. 4, 88, 90, 126, 258.

[8] Ibid., pp. 29, 82, 88, 89.

of action and reaction".[1] The term "Mind" is regularly used in reference to the human mind as a particular and as a class. However, it is also used in reference to God.[2]

In his later works Temple begins to define the category of mind more positively. In the Gifford Lectures mind is described as a process which appears within the universal process as a capacity for observing that process. In its generic sense mind is a new mode of being and activity which appears within the world process. This activity is distinguished by the fact that it is determined not by efficient causation or by simple response to stimuli but by the lure of apparent good, the appetitive appreciation of presented or imagined value. This activity consists of the calculation of means to an end presented as good.[3] This definition of the generic term amounts to a description of mind at its lowest stage of development, animal mind. Human mind (sometimes called spirit) is distinguished from animal mind in that it is capable of choosing between ends by reference to an ideal standard of good and capable of being the subject of absolute obligation.[4]

Again there is considerable confusion in the Gifford Lectures in the use of the terms "mind" and "Mind". These two terms seem to be used almost interchangeably with the following meanings: the complete generic sense including animal, human, and divine mind, a generic sense including animal and human mind, a generic sense including human and divine mind, the human mind as a class, the human mind as a particular (singular and plural), the animal mind as a class, the animal mind as a particular (singular and plural), individual minds both animal and human, divine mind in a

[1] *Christ the Truth*, p. 4. Cf. its use in this generic sense, pp. 5, 39.

[2] Ibid., p. 52.

[3] *Nature, Man and God*, pp. 120, 473, 475, 489; cf. "Some Implications of Theism", p. 419; *Christianity in Thought and Practice*, p. 55.

[4] "Some Implications of Theism", p. 419; *Christ the Truth*, p. 5; *Nature, Man and God*, p. 475; *Christianity in Thought and Practice*, p. 56.

generic sense, and the divine mind as a particular.[1] The only distinction in usage appears to be that "Mind" is used more often in the various generic senses and in summary sections for emphasis. One reason for the confusion among the various generic senses is that it is not clear whether certain modes of activity typical of human mind can be ascribed to animal mind and to the divine mind. For example, the definition of animal mind given above indicates that its activity is directed towards value, at least the values of pleasure, comfort, and satisfaction. Yet in the final Gifford Lecture Temple concludes that it would be better to limit the use of value to human and (presumably) divine mind.[2] Furthermore, Temple goes on to imply that sub-human consciousness is not fitly called mind.[3] The result is that in the discussions of the structure of reality and value it is not clear whether Temple is referring to the fully developed mind of man or to mind as a mode or principle found in animals as well as in man, and whether or not these characteristics of mind can be referred to the divine mind. This and other points of confusion become crucial in the development of the first dialectical transition in the argument for theism in the Gifford Lectures.

Temple's view of mind is based on the results of modern science.[4] Mind has appeared late in the story of evolution. The world which is apprehended by mind is apprehended as having existed long before it was thus apprehended. Apprehension takes place within the world, not the world within apprehension, as the Cartesian tradition implied. Furthermore, the scientific study of organic life has demonstrated Whitehead's proposition that consciousness presupposes experience and not vice versa. Mind or consciousness and later

---

[1] For examples of this confusion of usage, see *Nature, Man and God*, pp. 120, 130, 132, 134, 149, 153, 156, 212f, 219ff, 249, 251, 256f, 280ff, 316, 384f.

[2] Ibid., pp. 516f.   [3] Ibid., p. 504.

[4] See Chapter 5.

self-consciousness arise in the interaction between the organism and its environment. The earliest forms of consciousness are emotional and sympathetic. This emergence of mind in the process which it apprehends implies that the process itself must be grounded in mind.[1] The fact that mind apprehends and appreciates the process out of which it arises reveals the correlation or kinship between mind and the process which is the essence of value.

Once mind or consciousness has appeared, it introduces novelties into the process. It delivers the organism from bondage to mere routine by basing present action on future events. Thus, a non-physical activity determines the behaviour of the organism. Mind first appears as an organ for the satisfaction of the physical needs of the organism by attention to the general qualities of objects in the environment. In its later stages mind detaches these general qualities from the objects and forms concepts which it can handle independently of the objects. Particular objects rarely exhibit any general quality in exact correspondence to the concept because of modifications caused by the presence of other general qualities. As a result conceptual thought is more precise than the experience from which it is abstracted.[2]

Temple believes that this habit of mind of thinking by means of concepts or real kinds makes difficult the intellectual appreciation of the continuity which marks the world process. Continuous becoming is the most familiar fact of experience, and the unsophisticated mind apprehends it constantly without any difficulty or perplexity. The conceptual habit of thought tends mistakenly to view process as a series of stages and easily falls prey to Zeno's paradoxes. When we pass from actual apprehension to reflection on this apprehension, we transform an experience in which process was essential into an unchanging object of attention. Thus, whatever is fixed in a concept is always to some extent removed from reality.

[1] See Chapter 11.   [2] *Nature, Man and God*, pp. 199ff.

The mind's conceptual treatment of reality vindicates itself in varying degrees in practice. Its adequacy varies inversely with the importance of the principle of individuality in the area of attention. In the mind's apprehension of process the real value of conceptual thought is actualized only when this thought is brought to bear again on the process originally apprehended. When conceptual thought is understood to be such an interim procedure, there is no difficulty in the proposition that normal experience is of process. Time as an abstraction which can be analysed into parts is unreal; what is real is the successiveness in apprehension and in the objects of apprehension.[1]

Thus, the basis of the free activity of mind and its most characteristic and distinguishing feature is its capacity to form concepts or "free ideas", as Temple calls them. Mind draws these ideas from its experience of its environment, but it can detach them from the original experience and direct its attention to them apart from any experiential occasion for doing so. Moreover, the mind can unite these free ideas in new combinations of which experience gives no illustrations. The mind can modify its environment to bring about new combinations of elements which existed previously only in thought. The mind can compare and choose between goods offered by actual circumstances and those apprehended only in ideas. Thus, by means of its free ideas the mind becomes partially independent of the process out of which it arises. It gains a freedom expressed chiefly in the direction of attention whereby it selects its own nutriment and thus its own course of development.[2]

Temple states that the first and most conspicuous feature of the free activity of mind is its detachment from successiveness. The mind can hold in a single comprehension a whole period of the process in which it is involved. The present is not an

[1] *Nature, Man and God*, pp. 114ff.
[2] Ibid., pp. 212, 230, 236, 244, 361, 384, 467, 487, 498, 504.

abstract point in time but it is "so much of the empirical process as is immediately apprehended",[1] and there is no limit to the duration which can be so apprehended. The mind is distressed by transitoriness and "*declares its own nature by demanding permanence*".[2] The mind achieves this permanence in science and in art. It formulates changeless principles which describe the course of the process, and it holds a certain period in a single apprehension so that the process so apprehended becomes a constituent of the non-successive experience achieved. Temple concludes from these observations that the conception of an "eternal now" or "moment eternal" is not contradictory, since it can be illustrated in principle.[3]

The most significant characteristic of mind is purpose which is directed toward value and brings the future to bear as the most important factor in the present. By means of its free ideas mind is enabled to seek in the future a goal in the light of which action is directed in the present.[4]

Temple finds the clue to the problem of human freedom in the freedom of thought which is based on the capacity of the mind to form free ideas. He defines freedom as "determination by what seems good as contrasted with determination by irresistible compulsion",[5] either mechanical or organic. Thus, the free ideas of the mind not only enable it to choose between ends offered to it but also constitute the means of that integration and control of disorderly desires which is true human freedom. As the free ideas develop and increase their scope, more and more of experience is unified. These ideas can be roughly classified under the scientific, aesthetic, and moral activities of mind, and they act as leading principles for the co-ordination of the personality.[6]

Temple's view of mind and its free ideas plays a large part in his theory of moral evil. Mind achieves a certain detachment from its basis in the physical organism by means of its

---

[1] Ibid., p. 203. [2] Ibid., p. 204. [3] Ibid., p. 206.
[4] Ibid., pp. 206f. [5] Ibid., p. 229. [6] Ibid., pp. 230, 236f, 244.

free ideas. It holds these ideas by means of its capacity of imagination and thus supplies itself with the images which are necessary to all thought. This power of imagination to offer particular instances of general qualities presents a great stimulus to desire which then becomes either aspiration or lust. The condition for the occurrence of exaggerated or misdirected desire is identical with the condition of all the higher accomplishments of human life. Desire is directed toward what appears to the mind to be good, and this apparent good depends on the condition of the mind. Because the human mind is finite, the apparent good usually differs from the real good. The mind attaches more importance to values which are actualized within itself than to those which are not, and it is unaware of many of the latter type. Thus, a necessary self-centredness becomes self-assertion which is moral evil.[1]

Finally, Temple finds in his theory of mind and its free ideas a basis for the possibility of survival of physical death. By means of its free ideas the mind detaches itself from the course of the natural process and enters upon a realm of its own. The mind increasingly organizes itself apart from the processes which control the body and becomes increasingly independent of the physiological aspect of the organism. By means of the concentration of attention the complete sacrifice of the interests of the organism as such can be attained. Because of this possibility of the life of the mind in independence of the physiological functions of the organism, Temple concludes that man, although not immortal, is capable of immortality.[2]

Some further aspects of Temple's view of mind in relation to process will be dealt with in connection with the analysis of the first dialectical transition of the argument for theism in the Gifford Lectures. Temple believes that the fullest development of that intercourse of mind and world process which is the life of thought is found in revelation.[3]

---

[1] *Nature, Man and God*, pp. 360ff, 366.
[2] Ibid., pp. 467f.   [3] See Chapter 9.

Temple was deeply influenced by the tradition of idealism. He states that the teacher who most influenced him was Edward Caird. The books which most influenced him were by Bosanquet and Royce. His logic is clearly dependent upon that of Bosanquet. His value theory owes much to Bradley. He states that his final metaphysical position is close to that of Bosanquet and Caird.[1] His reviewers have called him an absolute idealist, an objective idealist, and a personal idealist.[2] However, Temple claims specifically to reject idealism and to affirm realism.[3] The solution of this problem lies in the clarification of the terminology used.

Idealism and realism can be used in both metaphysical and epistemological senses which are related but distinct. Metaphysical or logical realism is opposed to nominalism and refers to theories which affirm the reality of universals or essences, such as found in Plato, the scholastics, and some modern realists such as Moore and Whitehead. Epistemological realism, sometimes called dualism, is opposed to epistemological idealism and refers to modern theories which affirm that perception is of the real world and that the objects of perception exist independently of that perception, as is, for example, held by the authors of *The New Realism* and the English realists, Moore, Russell, and Broad. Both metaphysical and epistemological realism are at one in holding the independent existence of the thing in question, whether it be forms, universals, or physical objects, but they originated in different historical periods and with reference to different philosophical problems.

Metaphysical idealism is opposed to materialism and refers

---

[1] *Nature, Man and God*, pp. x, 498; *Thoughts in War-Time*, p. 97.

[2] Alban G. Widgery, *Contemporary Thought of Great Britain* (London: Williams and Norgate, 1927), p. 218; Randolph Crump Miller, "Is Temple a Realist", *The Journal of Religion*, XIX (January 1939), p. 50; Ralph E. Stedman, review of *Nature, Man and God*, *The Hibbert Journal*, XXXIII (January 1935), p. 302; Daniel Evans, review of *Nature, Man and God*, *Christendom*, I (October 1935), p. 181.

[3] *Nature, Man and God*, pp. ix, 109, 198, 201, 476, 490, 497ff.

to theories which affirm the priority or predominance of mind or hold that reality is essentially an embodiment of mind or spirit. This term has been applied to Platonism and post-Kantian German and British idealism. Epistemological idealism, as opposed to epistemological realism, is the theory that the reality of the external world is its perceptibility or that the mind has no objects but its own ideas. In one form or another this is one of the common presuppositions of "modern" philosophy from Descartes on. Metaphysical and epistemological idealism have in common the emphasis on the predominance or priority of mind, but they do not necessarily accompany each other. Now it is clear that Temple's claim refers to the epistemological meaning of the terms. He is claiming to reject epistemological idealism and to affirm epistemological realism. He is led, however,

> to a position which in its positive content is almost identical with such an Idealism as that of Edward Caird or of Bernard Bosanquet, apart from the method of arriving at it. For after repudiating the priority of mind *qua* knowing subject as a precondition of the actuality of the objective world, we were led to reaffirm the priority of mind *qua* purposive as the only condition of the intelligibility of that same objective world.[1]

Temple's claim is that by rejecting epistemological idealism and by affirming epistemological realism he has arrived by a dialectical method at a position close to metaphysical idealism.[2] This situation leads to considerable confusion among his reviewers and commentators, some of whom apparently think that he was using these terms in their metaphysical senses only and thus that he was rejecting metaphysical idealism and affirming metaphysical realism.[3]

It remains to determine whether or not Temple can really maintain his claim to epistemological realism. Since he

---

[1] *Nature, Man and God*, p. 498; cf. p. 201.

[2] See David Elton Trueblood, *The Logic of Belief: An Introduction to the Philosophy of Religion* (New York: Harper and Brothers, 1942), p. vi.

[3] See, for example, Miller, loc cit., p. 44.

believes that the objects of perception exist independently of that perception and that apprehension is of the real world and not of the mind's ideas, he would seem to have maintained the basic propositions of epistemological realism. It has been pointed out, however, that one aspect of Temple's theory of the relation of mind and process seems to be irreconcilable with a realistic epistemology.[1] Temple's frequent statement that mind finds *itself* in its object[2] would seem to be epistemological idealism, because it suggests that the mind's objects are of the nature of mind. However, the problem is made difficult by Temple's confusing use of the term mind. For example, when he states that in the value relation mind finds itself in its object, it is not clear whether that which is found is human mind, divine mind, or a mode of activity common to all types of mind.

But Temple has two other ways of expressing this correspondence between mind and the world process. One is very general and employs such words as kinship, correspondence, correlation, at-homeness, fitting-together, and counterpart.[3] This may mean that the apprehending mind finds other minds in its object, but this would still be an epistemological idealism. Or it may mean that mind finds its own principles or characteristics or the counterpart of its own activities in the object, and this is the third way in which Temple expresses this relationship.[4] He states that in the value relation mind finds its logical structure and its purposive and emotional qualities in the object. This is entirely compatible with epistemological realism, since the objects of the mind are neither dependent for their existence upon the mind nor are

[1] Miller, loc. cit., p. 46; E. W. Edwards, review of *Nature, Man and God, Mind*, XLIV (April 1935), p. 241.

[2] *Christ the Truth*, p. 39; *Nature, Man and God*, pp. 149, 153, 155, 160, 164, 168, 193, 208, 218f, 247, 357, 368, 385, 427, 488.

[3] *Christ the Truth*, p. 29; *Nature, Man and God*, pp. 129f, 132, 148f, 152, 154f, 165ff, 190, 208, 218, 249f, 357, 385, 387, 488, 514.

[4] *Christ the Truth*, p. 39; *Nature, Man and God*, pp. 149f, 155, 165f, 427.

they simply mind themselves. This seems to be the real meaning of Temple's first two ways of expressing the relation of mind to the world process. In the summary statement which has been referred to above, Temple concludes:

> When I say that Mind finds itself or what is akin to itself in its object, I mean an experience which has two aspects: first, that it finds the counterpart of the principle of its own activities as for example the mathematical properties of mechanical combinations of forces or of aesthetic proportions; secondly, that with this discovery goes a feeling of being at home with the object, not lost or bewildered in presence of it.[1]

It has also been suggested that the idealism in Temple's earlier works is indicated by the fact that he seeks an explanation of the world in terms of the cognitive demands of mind or coherence and that he assumes that, if an explanation satisfies our minds, such an explanation there must be. The further suggestion is that this idealism is modified in his later works where it is affirmed that it is the volitional or purposive aspect of mind which supplies the key to the explanation of the world and that the mind makes a demand is not sufficient evidence that the universe must satisfy that demand but is only a venture of faith.[2] However, both of these suggestions seem to be erroneous. In Temple's earliest works on this subject he develops the idea that coherence alone is inadequate as an explanatory principle and that it is the purposive aspect of mind which offers a satisfactory explanation of the world.[3] Also, in his earliest works Temple makes it clear that any explanatory principle suggested by the demands of mind is only a hypothesis or a venture of faith.[4]

---

[1] *Nature, Man and God*, p. 165.

[2] Emmet, "The Philosopher", in Iremonger, op cit., pp. 527f.

[3] *The Faith and Modern Thought*, pp. 16ff; *The Nature of Personality*, p. xxiv; *The Kingdom of God*, p. 108; *Mens Creatrix*, pp. 22, 89, 258.

[4] *The Faith and Modern Thought*, p. 18; *Mens Creatrix*, pp. 89, 258.

9

RELIGIOUS EXPERIENCE, AUTHORITY, AND REVELATION

SINCE Temple believes that the enterprise of natural theology should include the investigation of the actual religions of mankind, an important aspect of his philosophy of religion is his interpretation of religious experience. Since authority is apparently a universal element in religion, its place and function in religion and religious experience is a question to be investigated by natural theology. The problem of religious experience raises the question of religious knowledge, the question of knowledge of the religious object which is alleged to be the source of religious experience. Temple's dialectical argument for theism leads him to one of the classical answers to the question of religious knowledge, the divine self-disclosure or revelation.

Temple's approach to religious experience is by way of a criticism of a view which has prevailed among psychologists and philosophers of religion. This view has tended to associate the phrase, religious experience, with extraordinary moments of intense awareness of the presence of God, such as visions, trances, ecstacies, sudden experiences of conversion, and other mystical states, which happen only rarely in the lives of a relatively small number of people. William James' famous Gifford Lectures encouraged this tendency to isolate such experiences and to confine the meaning of the phrase, religious experience, to them. It is Temple's contention that such momentary experiences do not constitute the whole or even the chief or indispensable part of religious experience. Rather they are merely outstanding moments which focus the inner meaning of a whole way of life. If they stood alone, they would be of relatively small importance. They derive their importance from the fact that they are focuses of a quality which permanently pervades the whole life of a religious person and supplies the background of all his experience. Religion is not a department of life; it claims life as a whole for its sphere. The religious person is religious not only during such momentary experiences but in all moments and activities of his life.[1]

Thus, Temple defines religious experience as the whole experience of religious persons, the whole reaction to circumstances resulting from belief in God and an acknowledged relationship to him, the whole experience of life and the world permeated through and through with religion. Religious experience is a person's experience of communion with a single ruling power in whose hands he is, who is intimate with him and his inmost thoughts, and who encompasses, guides, and upholds him. It is always an experience of finding something which is given and objective.[2]

The necessary basis of such experience according to Temple is divine immanence, the activity of God in the world process. However, the validity of religious experience is challenged as no other type of experience is. Some psychological interpretations of religion hold that religious experience is purely subjective with no counterpart in the objective world. Psychological theories range from self-hypnosis and auto-suggestion to projection or compensation as sources of religious experience. Religious experience is often interpreted as a psychic reaction to a certain type of treatment in infancy or as a projection in compensation for the non-realization of certain aspirations.

---

[1] *The Faith and Modern Thought*, p. 7; *Studies in the Spirit and Truth of Christianity*, pp. 27ff, 62, 66; "Some Implications of Theism", pp. 424f; *Christ the Truth*, pp. 43f; *Nature, Man and God*, pp. 334f; *Religious Experience*, p. 60.

[2] *The Faith and Modern Thought*, pp. 7, 19, 27f, 31; *Studies in the Spirit and Truth of Christianity*, p. 66; *Mens Creatrix*, p. 259; *Christ the Truth*, pp. 44, 47; *Nature, Man and God*, pp. 334f.

Temple meets this line of argument by the assertion of a realistic epistemology and by accusing the psychologists of unscientific bias or of the genetic fallacy. If one holds a realistic epistemology with reference to most normal experiences, there is no *a priori* reason for not applying it in the case of religious experience and denying the objective reference of such experience. Religious experience needs to be criticized and interpreted to purify it of illusion and hallucinations, but this is true of all forms of experience. Apprehension is of reality, and there is no ground for treating religious experience as less veridical than any other experience unless there is an original bias against the theistic interpretation of the world. The burden of proof rests on those who would arbitrarily mark off one area of experience as illusory. This procedure in fact opens the gate to a radical scepticism which can end only in solipsism.

However, psychologists must follow the sound scientific principle of attempting to account for any set of data in terms of the lowest possible category and not adopt a higher category of explanation until all the possibilities of explanation by lower categories are exhausted. Thus, it will be a long time indeed before psychology as a science can be so sure of having exhausted the possibilities of a purely psychological origin of religious experience, that it can safely admit the hypothesis that it is due to the action of God (a being necessarily unknown to psychology) on the human mind. If a psychologist develops a scheme for explaining how religious experience and religious convictions arise in the mind and concludes as a result that they are illusory, he is making an unscientific philosophical speculation. It may be possible in a similar way to explain how his theory arose in his mind and to conclude that it also is illusory. If a history of its growth can be used to discredit a theological belief, it may also be used to discredit a psychological belief. When one area of experience is considered illusory, the way is opened to a scepticism which declares all experience to be illusory.

Furthermore, Temple believes that such a psychological theory and conclusion is an example of the genetic fallacy. The theory may be correct and still it will be completely irrelevant to the question of the existence of God. Some religious experience may be completely illusory, and yet a conviction based on it may be true. In his earlier works Temple also makes the point that since the general philosophical argument tends to a theistic conclusion, serious attention should be paid to the type of experience which suggests the same conclusion.[1] Although in his later works he is somewhat more tentative about the conclusion of the general philosophical argument, he still maintains that the case for theism depends on a convergence of the philosophical argument and religious experience.[2]

Temple believes that religious experience is almost universal but also incommunicable. It is universal in the sense that few people if any go through life without ever feeling reverence for something which is morally so high above them as to be out of reach, or awe before the great reality on which they are utterly dependent, or feeling the sense of absolute obligation. All of these are religious experiences, because they are the recognition of an absolute. Religious experience is incommunicable in the same sense that value is. The only way in which a person can understand and appreciate it is to have such an experience.[3]

The form of religious experience develops through various stages in the history of culture. In the primitive stage of development subjective and objective factors are not distinguished, and perception and interpretation are fused. At this stage it is the sense of vastness and power which constitutes

---

[1] *The Faith and Modern Thought*, pp. x-xiii, 4–7; *Mens Creatrix*, pp. 259f, 357f; *Christ the Truth*, pp. 45ff; *Nature, Man and God*, p. 50; *The Church and Its Teaching Today*, p. 31.

[2] *Christ the Truth*, pp. 46, 113, 208; *Nature, Man and God*, p. 265.

[3] *The Faith and Modern Thought*, pp. 4, 7, 25, 27f; *Studies in the Spirit and Truth of Christianity*, p. 70; *Christ the Truth*, pp. 47, 50, 113f, 208.

religious experience. Man feels small and helpless in the face of a vast world supposed to be animated with unknown powers, and he associates divine activity with unusual manifestations of natural forces. Progress begins with an awareness of the divine apart from any particular external occasion. It is only at a later stage that value as well as power becomes associated with the divine.

During the historic period development has come through the religious experience of individuals and through the philosophical reflection of individuals. The religious experience of large groups, although effective in strengthening the common faith, is almost certain to conform closely to the prevailing religious tradition. The classical case of the purgation of the religious tradition by philosophical reflection is Xenophanes, who criticized the tradition in the light of the ethical consciousness of the community. Philosophers have helped to purge the religious tradition of superstition and moral contradiction and to expand the thought of God so that it will be more adequately related to secular knowledge, but the growth and development of religion comes from the religious experience of individuals.

Although individual religious experience is conditioned by the tradition, it may go beyond it. A vivid apprehension of certain aspects of the tradition may bring them into new prominence, cause others to decrease in importance or drop out, and thus transform the tradition itself. Examples of such transformation are the accomplishments of the eighth century B.C. Hebrew prophets and the change of status of the Levitical love commandment as it appears in the teaching of Jesus. The religious experience on which these transformations were based was a communion of the divine and human spirits, but it was mediated by the tradition and by events in the contemporary world.[1]

Temple distinguishes two main traditions of religious

---

[1] *Christ the Truth*, p. 43; *Nature, Man and God*, pp. 328f, 336–41.

experience, one emphasizing intellectual and the other moral interests. The intellectual tradition with its concern for totality leads to a conception of God or ultimate reality as the absolute one. This type issues in religious experience which aims at a mystical union in which the distinction between man and God disappears. The other tradition leads to a conception of God who is active, purposive, and creative. This tradition issues in religious experience typified by a personal communion in which the human divine distinction is never lost.[1]

It is in the latter tradition in which God is understood as creative will that religious experience is associated with value. Reference has already been made to Temple's statement that experience of value is essentially a religious experience. He contends that the sense of absolute obligation which accompanies the apprehension of absolute value is the most universal form of religious experience. The obligation deriving from the absolute value of truth and beauty is a true religious experience, but it is the obligation deriving from goodness which is most universal, because goodness is the specifically human value.[2]

In one sense the form of religious experience which an individual will have is determined by himself, his character, and the stage of his religious development. But in another and more important sense the form of an individual's religious experience is dependent upon the religious tradition in which he stands and which has made him what he is. The subjective or internal and the objective or external factors determining the form of religious experience are always found together, but the objective and external factors are always prior in importance. For example, Luther's religious experience enabled him to free himself from the medieval religious tradition, but his experience was informed by the Pauline tradition as preserved in the New Testament. However, although the individual's religious experience depends on the religious

---

[1] *Nature, Man and God*, pp. 329ff.　　[2] *Christ the Truth*, pp. 42, 47f, 114.

tradition, in the totality of religious history, as has been noted above, tradition depends upon experience.[1]

The nature of religious experience and its relation to religious tradition raises the problem of authority in religion. Temple believes that authority is a universal, indispensable, and essential element in all living religion.

> Consciousness of authority and submission to it is the very heart of true religion. It is because of this that religious history is so full of tragic submission to authority of the wrong kind, and of consequent reactions in which men try to practice religion apart from authority and fall into every variety of phantasy. The heart of religion, as has repeatedly been emphasized, is acknowledgement by the finite of insignificance before the Infinite, by the sinner of pollution before the Holy, by the creature of total dependence before the Creator. It is in its essence a submission to authority.[2]

The authoritative character of religion is presented to the individual in various ways in the different stages of his religious development. In the primitive stage of religious development, as has been noted above, authority and experience are indistinguishably fused. At a later stage when authority and experience become distinct, they are found to be mutually interdependent.

> The supposed conflict between Authority and Experience in religion is really a tension between two indispensable elements. For the individual Authority, whether as tribal custom or as alleged Revelation, is prior to Experience; in the race as a whole Experience is prior to Authority.[3]

Religious authority presents itself to the individual in two ways: in the religious tradition of his social environment, and in personal experience of the divine. If there is any divergence in these two types of authority, the initial presumption is

[1] *The Faith and Modern Thought*, pp. 33, 35; *Nature, Man and God*, pp. 331ff, 335f.
[2] *Nature, Man and God*, p. 343; cf. pp. 18ff, 23, 249, 329.
[3] Ibid., p. 329.

7

always in favour of the tradition since it represents the deposit of many individual experiences. But the tradition as a whole has been formed by many such individual experiences, and the growth and development of the tradition comes primarily from these experiences.

In the religious development of the individual authority in the form of some tradition is usually prior to the authority of experience. Early religious belief is formed on the basis of external authority such as parents, teachers, or friends. There is no difference here between a child brought up by religious parents and an adult converted by a preacher. In both cases it is a matter of surrender or submission to authority. Gradually there comes a shift in the basis of belief to personal experience, reflection, and criticism, and with this shift the individual becomes independent of this type of external authority and gains a real autonomy. But this growth of religious conviction which makes the individual independent of human authority brings him into an ever closer relation with a being who claims the allegiance of his entire nature. Thus, the individual is not delivered *from* authority but to an authority of a new kind. He has reached a personal conviction of the existence of a God who is entitled to exercise absolute authority over him. The authoritative element in religion increases as the religious life matures, although it changes from the authority of the mediator of belief to the authority of the object of belief. The indestructible note of authority in the object of religious belief has recently been emphasized by Rudolph Otto and by the theologians of the school of Barth and Brunner.[1]

Temple believes that in none of the stages of religious development is authority necessarily set against reason. Reason is not to be contrasted with authority but is a necessary element in authority. It is impossible to accept a belief

[1] *Nature, Man and God*, pp. 18ff, 23, 329, 343f; *The Church and Its Teaching Today*, p. 26.

on authority except so far as the authority is accepted by reason. If a child's acceptance of a belief is totally uncritical, it is not acceptance on authority but on the causal action of the impressions received. His belief rests on authority only when his acceptance of it is due to his trust in those who present it to him. In the case of the adult whose religious belief involves submission to the authority of the object of his belief, such submission is in accord with reason, since the object of his belief is the source and ground of his reason. The ages of persecution have given us an idea of authority which is identified with compulsion. But the proper meaning of authority is an appeal to reason in respect of the right of authority to command acceptance.[1]

True spiritual authority requires free acceptance, because the essence of spirituality is freedom. Spirit is controlled not by force or physical causation but by the good in one of its forms. This control by the good becomes operative only through appreciation by the spirit subject to it. "Consequently *the essential principle of spiritual authority is the evocation by Good of appreciation of itself: for only when this occurs is authority exercised over the spirit.*"[2] Spiritual authority operates in the sphere of the discovery by spirit of itself or what is akin to itself in its object which is the essential condition of actual value. A man may act in a certain way out of loyalty to his religious group without being persuaded that the act is right. Such an act may be fully spiritual in quality, because it is based on a conviction that conformity is good, although the justification of the particular act is not understood. This, however, is a limitation of the area of full spiritual response, and the response is always more fully spiritual when the particular act is recognized as good.

There are various degrees of approximation to true spiritual freedom according to the degree in which any act is truly

---

[1] *Nature, Man and God*, pp. 7, 19n, 20; *The Church and Its Teaching Today*, p. 26.

[2] *Nature, Man and God*, p. 345.

voluntary, and if determinants of choice other than the good in and for itself are involved, we have something less than spiritual freedom. Authority does not become spiritual because it is exercised by a spiritual being. When a person is incapable of response to the appeal of the good, God may be understood as using an appeal to fear of impending doom, for example, to bring about conformity to a divine command. A truly spiritual being will have recourse to such methods only as preparatory to the exercise of truly spiritual authority. The spiritual authority of God is not exercised by displaying his omnipotence but rather his holiness, not in having power to create and destroy but in being the appropriate object of worship and love. Temple concludes:

> The true contrast, then, is not between religions of the spirit and religions of authority, for authority may be fully spiritual and cannot be truly authority at all if it be not partly spiritual; there is no proper authority in physical compulsion, or coercion by fear, or inducement by bribery. The true contrast is between the authority which exacts deference through its own inherent quality, and that which exacts deference through any non-spiritual form of sanction.[1]

The spiritual nature of the authority of any alleged divine self-disclosure or disclosure of the divine will can be maintained only if the response to it is based on an exercise of private judgement because this is the essentially spiritual principle. Thus, in whatever degree reliance upon infallible knowledge or guidance enters into religion, spirituality and spiritual authority go out because private judgement is denied.

Temple's critical realism in regard to the problem of religious knowledge has been described. Religious experience in its cognitive aspect gives knowledge of God. All knowledge is directly or indirectly knowledge of God, because it is knowledge of the world created by God. Also, science may be considered an intercourse between the mind of man and the

---

[1] *Nature, Man and God*, pp. 348f.   [2] Ibid., pp. 345-53.

divine mind expressed in the universe. But the knowledge of God deriving from the knowledge of the world is very different from the knowledge of God which comes in religious experience. The first is the result of observation and reflection, but the second is the knowledge of a personal relationship. The contrast is similar to that between the knowledge gained from a description of a picture or a person and that gained from seeing the picture or meeting the person. Also, belief in God results primarily from religious experience rather than intellectual arguments for theism based on scientific knowledge of the world.[1]

Temple believes that the dominant problem of contemporary religious thought is the problem of divine revelation: whether there is any such thing, and, if there is, what is its mode and form. His own position is that the apprehension and appreciation of revelation is the special form of religious experience which gives knowledge of the personal God. The basis of the possibility of revelation is in the personal nature of God and in the nature of his relationship to the world process. If the ultimate principle were understood as being nonpersonal, no occurrences could be interpreted as purposive self-revelations of that principle. In the second dialectical transition of the argument for theism in the Gifford Lectures Temple claims to establish the personal nature of God. If God is personal, then he can only be known through his own self-revelation, and not only is he revealed in the world process which is the product of his creative will, but also he is capable of special acts of self-revelation. Thus, for Temple revelation is the solution of the problem of religious knowledge.[2]

Temple describes the relation of God to the world process in terms of transcendence and immanence. He states his theory in criticism of a view commonly held by theologians and

[1] *The Faith and Modern Thought*, pp. 30ff; *The Church and Its Teaching Today*, pp. 9, 49, 208.

[2] *Nature, Man and God*, pp. 264, 299f, 328; *The Church and Its Teaching Today*, pp. 43f; *Revelation*, p. 83.

religious philosophers of the late nineteenth and early twentieth centuries. The successes of the natural sciences had given great weight to the postulate of the uniformity of nature. Yielding to this pressure these religious thinkers tried to relate this postulate to the belief in the personal nature of God. They did this by taking the laws of nature to be the mode of divine immanence and by positing a divine transcendence whereby God could intervene and modify his normal constancy of action by the occasional exercise of a reserve of power in acts called miracles. They held that God created the world and imposed laws upon it which it follows unless he intervenes. This led to the criticism that it would be more fitting if God in his infinite wisdom and power would impose laws which would never need modification.

Temple, however, believes that constancy of action is not so representative of personality as is constancy of purpose. This shows itself not in unalterable uniformity of conduct but in perpetual adaptation to varying circumstances so that the unchanging purpose is furthered. Thus, laws of nature are not ultimate but are general statements of that course of the world process which normally fulfills the purpose of God. Since intelligent, purposive, and moral action depends upon the constancy of the natural processes, a large degree of uniformity in the world process might be expected. But when circumstances require it, constancy of purpose may be expressed in variations in an infinite gradation from the norm. When a variation is such as to attract attention, it is called a miracle. Miracles, however, are no more the manifestation of God immanent than are the regular processes of nature.[1]

God is not immanent in the universe as a carpenter is in a box he has made or an inventor in a machine he has produced. God is not outside the universe and acting on it from without; he is its informing and vitalizing principle. Nor is God immanent in the world as a poet is in his poems. This

---

[1] *Nature, Man and God*, pp. 266f, 286f, 292ff, 299, 315.

still makes God too external to the world. The classic case of immanence, that of mind in body, if applied to divine immanence, easily leads to a parallelism of God and world similar to that of Whitehead in which God and world are completely correlative.[1] This leaves the totality of God plus world unexplained. Temple contends that God and the world are not correlative. Rather God as immanent is correlative with the world; but that is not the whole nature of God. He is also transcendent, as personality must always be in relation to process. A person is truly immanent only in his conduct, and yet he also transcends his conduct. His special identity is expressed in the difference in his conduct in different circumstances. Therefore, the personal God must be related to the world process as a man is related to his actions. This relation of transcendence and immanence of the person or the personal God to his actions involves "that infinite delicacy of adjustment to varying conditions in which purposive as distinct from mechanical or chemical action consists".[2]

Therefore, the world process in which the personal God is immanent cannot be unalterably determined but must be open to determination by God. The action and reaction of all the parts of the world process are determined at every moment by the wisdom of God. But this variability of the world process which is required by the divine personality does not introduce chaos or caprice into the universe, because the divine personality is also transcendent and unchanging. The immanent activity may vary, but the transcendent being is eternally the same. *"God immanent is a principle or energy of adjustment and therefore of variation: God transcendent is the eternally self-identical —the I AM."*[3]

Since the God who stands in such a relation of transcendence

---

[1] *Process and Reality*, p. 492; quoted, *Nature, Man and God*, p. 273.

[2] *Nature, Man and God* p. 284.

[3] Ibid., p. 295; cf. also pp. 265f, 269f, 283–6, 289f, 292f, 297–300, 302, 313; *Christ the Truth*, pp. 118–21; *The Church and Its Teaching Today*, pp. 45f; *Revelation*, pp. 92f, 108.

and immanence to the world process is personal, the whole world process is the expression of his activity. All occurrences are in some degree a revelation of God. And presumably the entire course of cosmic history would afford a full self-revelation of God. But since no one could contemplate this history in its entirety, this could not constitute a full self-revelation for any human being. Also, the distortion of perspective caused by man's self-centredness makes the full and perfect reception of the revelation in the world process impossible. Temple emphasizes the universality of revelation as the necessary basis of the possibility of particular or special revelation. Only if God is personal can there be any special revelation, and if he is personal, then all existence is revelation. Temple refers to this revelation in all existence as the general revelation of the attributes of God. But, although God discloses himself in the uniformities of nature and this revelation is perfect in its kind, it is incomplete and inadequate, because the personal God cannot fully reveal himself through anything sub-personal.[1]

While personality is immanent and revealed in all conduct, it is not equally expressed in all. It is more adequately revealed in those unusual situations and special circumstances which require a departure from the normal activity. These occasional variations are peculiarly revealing, because they are the issue of a specially directed activity. Both the choice of occasion for unusual action and the mode of action taken are especially revealing. This unusual action is not the manifestation of a new and usually dormant power but is simply the continuing personal purpose being carried out in a way demanded by the circumstances. Thus, the full self-revelation of God will come in the special activity which is in response to critical situations. Temple states that since God is personal, there is more ground in reason for expecting such specially

---

[1] *Nature, Man and God*, pp. 266, 290, 293f, 296, 302, 304-7, 314, 349; *The Church and Its Teaching Today*, p. 45; *Revelation*, pp. 95-8.

revealing activity than for denying it. "So intimately bound up in one another are the Personality of the Ultimate and specific acts of revelation that an *a priori* argument for the former would be highly precarious if not supported by the latter."[1] The critical situations which would produce this specially revealing activity arise primarily as a result of the activities of human free agents. It is always in dealing with persons that personality expresses itself most fully. Therefore, the main area of divine revelation will be the history of men.[2]

Furthermore, the personal God could be adequately and fully revealed only through the life of a person, because the revelation is to persons who can fully understand only what is personal. If the person who is the medium of the revelation is to be adequate to this function, he must be one in essence with the God whom he reveals.[3]

Temple proceeds to discuss the forms that religious people have supposed special revelation to have taken, how far they are philosophically justifiable, and what the conditions would be of a fully satisfactory revelation. He begins with a criticism of the traditional interpretation of revelation in Christianity. This traditional doctrine has been that the Bible itself is the revelation rather than the events recorded in the Bible. This position as stated in the Vatican Decrees of 1870 and re-affirmed in 1893 in the Encyclical *Providentissimus Deus* of Leo XIII holds that the Bible is absolutely inerrant because it was "written wholly and entirely . . . at the dictation of the Holy Ghost". In other words, God has so overridden and superseded the normal human faculties of those through whom the revelation was given that their utterances are saved from all error. This Temple believes to be inconsistent with the content of the revelation so given. The Bible describes God as empowering men to do his will by enlightening

---

[1] *Nature, Man and God*, pp. 264f.

[2] Ibid., pp. 296f, 302, 305, 307, 314f; *Christ the Truth*, pp. 120f; *Revelation*, pp. 93f.

[3] *Nature, Man and God*, pp. 266, 305, 319, 321f.

and enabling their natural faculties rather than by the super-session of them. The historical figure who is the culmination of the revelation is pictured as having unfailing respect for the spiritual liberty of those with whom he dealt. His teaching was designed to stimulate thought rather than to supersede it by supplying formulated doctrines to be accepted on his authority. Furthermore, the fathers of the Church, such as Augustine and Aquinas, found recourse to the allegorical method of interpretation necessary in order to avoid the con-tradictions resulting from a literal interpretation. They held that the Bible was inerrant but that it could be interpreted in many senses. Temple points out, however, that this theory is not consistent. It is impossible to hold that a revelation is inerrant, if it is impossible to determine which interpretation is the true one. Unless the revelation is both inerrant and un-mistakable, it fails in its function of imparting truth. One method of overcoming this difficulty is to accept only the literal meaning and to attempt to explain away all the result-ing contradictions. The other is to move from the infallible book to the infallible Church as interpreter of the book and finally to the infallible spokesman of the infallible Church.

There is another way in which the traditional theory is not consonant with the content of the revelation. The theory im-plies that the content of the revelation is propositions about God and his works, authoritative declarations of theological doctrine, whereas the Bible contains very little of this. This aspect of the theory is due to the false estimate of conceptual thought held by Greek, Scholastic, and Cartesian philosophers. Temple's view is that conceptual thought is an interim pro-cedure which corresponds to analytical study of the score between two occasions of hearing great music. He concludes: "*there is no such thing as revealed truth. There are truths of revelation, that is to say propositions which express the result of correct thinking concerning revelation; but they are not themselves directly revealed.*"[1]

---

[1] *Nature, Man and God*, p. 317; cf. pp. 308–12, 316f, 322; *Revelation*, pp. 100ff, 120f; *Religious Experience*, p. 235.

As against this traditional theory of revelation, Temple states the view of revelation which follows from the conception of the universe to which his reflections have led him. Revelation consists of the appreciation of divinely guided historical events by divinely illumined minds. It is not the communication of doctrinal truths but the

> living apprehension of a living process wherein those whose minds are enlightened by divine communion can discern in part the purposive activity of God. . . . *He guides the process; He guides the minds of men; the interaction of the process and the minds which are alike guided by Him is the essence of revelation.*[1]

Thus, revelation is the fullest development of the intercourse between mind and the world process in which value consists and the fullest actuality of the relationship between nature, man, and God which Temple is attempting to articulate in all of his thought. Here the mind which arises in the process apprehends the process for what it really is: the expression and self-disclosure of the divine mind. Like the apprehension of value, revelation occurs objectively but is subjectively received and conditioned. Revelation is not something belonging purely to the subject world, such as truth or ideas immediately apprehended, but it is mediated by historical events. But revelation must be appreciated and received in order to be revelation. If no one were to apprehend a divinely guided event as such, it would not be revelatory.[2]

Temple believes that all positive religions make some kind of a claim of divine revelation. This raises the problem of the authentication of revelation and the determination of which is the true revelation. By the nature of the case revelation must be self-authenticating. If it had to appeal to a criterion outside itself, this criterion would itself be the revelation. The traditional Christian interpretation of revelation found authentication in miracle and fulfilled prediction. In

[1] *Nature, Man and God*, p. 312.
[2] Ibid., pp. 305, 312, 314ff, 318, 322, 241; *Revelation*, pp. 100f, 103, 106ff.

themselves these things are irrelevant to the authenticity of revelation, but when taken as examples of broader principles they are justified. When miracles are understood as manifestations of the divine purpose in special situations, and when the fulfilment of prophecy is understood as progress in the divine self-disclosure toward a more complete convergence of various lines of development, these things may be considered evidence for the truth of revelation. The marks of a true revelation are

> a union of holiness and power, before which our spirits bow in awe, and which authenticates itself by continuous development to some focal point in which all preparatory revelation finds fulfilment, and from which illumination radiates into every department of life and being.[1]

Thus, the true revelation will provide at least the source and starting point of a more satisfactory philosophy of life and of the universe than we can frame without it.

The religions of the East have sacred writings for which there is a claim to inspiration. But this claim is not damaged by the admission that the stories in these writings are legendary. For the emphasis in these religions is laid on the truth of the ideas, and whatever imparts true ideas is adequate revelation. Temple believes that such revelation is purely subjective and does not hold the balance between subjective and objective which is necessary for a true revelation. It takes place in the mind of man without reference to external events. Only in Islam is a claim made for revelation in the Koran which appears to fulfil the qualifications for a true revelation. But Temple points out that the revelation in this case is not in Mohammed but in his message, and therefore it also is over-subjective and consists mainly of precepts. Temple concludes that the revelation of the positive religions other than Christianity is embodied in precepts or customs which do not

---

[1] *Nature, Man and God*, pp. 324f.

do justice to the necessary objectivity of true revelation. These may be real revelations, but they are necessarily partial.[1]

The authoritative quality of a religious tradition is at a maximum where the tradition contains special revelation. Thus, the problem of spiritual authority is raised most acutely in connection with revelation. Revelation is essentially a personal disclosure to persons and has authority as a demand for personal loyalty. In the Hebrew-Christian tradition God is revealed as holy and righteous love, and the acceptance of such revelation is not primarily in intellectual assent but in submission of will. If the authority mediated in revelation is to be spiritual, it must be accepted by a free act of private judgement which is an appreciation of the goodness of him who is revealed. It must avoid both intellectual coercion by irresistible evidence and coercion by appeal to anything less than appreciation of good.

It follows that the authority of revelation is never decisive for anyone except him who receives it. In the case of a prophetic oracle the divine control of the subjective and objective factors is mediated by the prophet's personality and religious history including the religious tradition in which he matured. As a result the divine and human factors are inextricably intermingled, and the degree of human distortion of the divine is indeterminate. Furthermore, such an oracle has direct application only to one particular occasion, and it is impossible to determine how far it applies to any other occasion. This, however, is the only way to true universality; not through a code of general principles which must become more abstract as their sphere of application is enlarged, but through the manifestation of the spirit of a divine-human communion which gives the basis of the approach to any situation. Temple calls this artistic as against scientific universality and gives as an example the universality of Christ:

[1] *Nature, Man and God*, pp. 323f, 344; *Revelation*, pp. 99f, 116ff, 122f.

Because the authority to which we submit is a person, not a code of rules, there is no conceivable set of circumstances in which loyalty to Him will not control us or the love of Christ constrain us; because he never legislated, He can be a source of direction for every phase of civilization; because his utterances are strictly occasional, every one is of universal import.[1]

[1] *Revelation*, p. 110; cf. pp. 114ff, 118–22; *Nature, Man and God*, pp. 328, 331, 341ff, 351, 354.

10

HISTORY AND ETERNITY

TEMPLE approaches the interpretation of history from the point of view of his theory of value. Since history, subjectively considered, is the apprehension and interpretation of events, it is an activity of mind which combines the three mental activities, intellectual, aesthetical, and ethical, which are the subjective counterparts of the three ultimate values, truth, beauty, and goodness. The historian must ascertain the truth about the facts. He must also present the facts so as to exhibit their significance, and this calls for the aesthetic or artistic activity of mind. Finally, his selection of the facts must be governed by a principle which is a judgement of moral value.[1]

Objectively considered, history is the sum total of events, and the relation of these events and their totality to what is real but other than event is the problem of history as Temple poses it. The two value-appreciating activities of mind, science and art, point to a common culmination in "a perfect grasp of the entire Universe in all its extent of space and time by an Eternal Mind. . . . If we could grasp all history in a single apprehension that would be the culmination alike of science and art."[2] Thus, for Temple the problem of history becomes the problem of the relation between history and eternity.

Temple's views on the relation between history and eternity are based on a critique of other views of this relation which over-emphasize either the eternal or the temporal. The former view is that the eternal is independent of the temporal which proceeds from it and expresses it. History is the temporal presentation of a self-subsistent eternal reality. This is the

---

[1] *Nature, Man and God*, pp. 427f.   [2] *Mens Creatrix*, pp. 126f.

Platonic teaching that time is the moving image of eternity. An extreme version of this view would declare that history or the temporal is illusory. Temple believes that this renders history meaningless, because it supplies no ground for its existence, although it may supply an explanation of the content of history. In the second transition of his argument for theism Temple affirms that such a doctrine of thoroughgoing transcendence is necessary to make the universe explicable. This may give history meaning in that it is an expression of eternity, but it gives history no ultimate meaning, that is, no meaning for eternity. Thus, the eternal production of the temporal becomes meaningless. Transcendence must be balanced by immanence if history is to have meaning for eternity. The extreme view that history is illusory becomes involved in the logical difficulty that our apprehension of the illusory character of the temporal is also part of the illusion.[1]

The alternative view is that eternity is the integral totality of history, the sum-total of the temporal simultaneously apprehended. This view appears to give ultimate significance to history, for history actually constitutes the content of eternity. (It also solves the problem of evil by affirming that what appears evil will contribute in the course of history to the completion of the total good.) But this view causes eternity to be dependent upon our moral action, and Temple believes this "apotheosis of Pelagianism" to be insupportable. While the exclusive concern for the eternal may give both the eternal and the temporal some provisional meaning, the exclusive concern for the temporal renders both meaningless. "The successive as such cannot display meaning."[2]

Temple also rejects what he describes as the naïve religious view of the relation between history and eternity. Here history is episodic to eternity. The eternal is constant but

[1] *Christ the Truth*, p. 107; *Personal Religion and the Life of Fellowship*, pp. 15f; *Nature, Man and God*, pp. 429, 434ff.

[2] *Nature, Man and God*, p. 430; cf. pp. 429, 434, 437f; *Christ the Truth*, p. 107.

initiates the temporal which somehow returns to it. This view recognizes the supremacy of the eternal and the significance of the historical, but the relation between eternity and history is external to both. There is not sufficient reason for the eternal to have launched the temporal. Eternity is not clearly transcendent nor is history of ultimate importance to eternity.[1]

Temple defines eternity in relation to history as "an experience that should include in a single apprehension the whole course of Time, even though that course be endless in both directions", and as "a unitary synthetic apprehension of the whole process of Time and all that happens in it".[2]

Temple's view of the relation between history and eternity is dialectical. "As we must regard history in the light of eternity, so we must conceive eternity in the light of history. History and eternity must be so conceived as to interpret each other."[3] The significance of a process may lie in its result or in its whole course or in both. The meaning of history cannot lie entirely in its result, because only those alive at the end would participate in this meaning, and this would be morally irrational. If the meaning of history lies partly in the process, it can be apprehended only from a point of view outside the process from which the process can be regarded as a single whole, that is, from the point of view of eternity. But "eternity must be conceived as requiring the actual historic process as part of its own content".[4]

Temple attempts to hold together the complete supremacy and transcendence of the eternal and the ultimate importance of the historical. Eternity is affected by history. In one sense history makes no difference to eternity, because the latter is not successive. "But in another sense History makes a great difference to the Eternal; for if there were no History, or if

---

[1] *Nature, Man and God*, pp. 434, 438ff.
[2] *Mens Creatrix*, p. 357; *Christ the Truth*, p. 223.
[3] *Christ the Truth*, p. 107.   [4] Ibid.

History were other than in fact it is, the Eternal would not
be what the Eternal is."[1] There is complete disparity as to
dependence between the eternal and the historical, but the
historical is a necessary self-expression of the eternal.

> *The eternal is the ground of the historical, and not* vice versa; *but
> the relation is necessary, not contingent—essential, not incidental.*

> The Eternal is self-expressed in History; but this act of self-
> expression is not epiphenomenal to the Eternal—a mere by-
> product of its own unmoved perfection. The Eternal fulfils
> itself in its historical self-expression, so that if this were abolished,
> it would in its own nature be other than it is.[2]

The values found in the historical belong essentially to the
eternal, and in some measure constitute the richness of the
eternal.

Temple declares, however, that the finite human mind cannot form a wholly adequate conception of eternity and its
relation to history. The method here can be only one of analogy,[3] and the two which Temple suggests are the piece of
music or drama and the father of a family.

When a person hears a symphony with which he is familiar,
he perceives a real development of the themes. At the end of
the symphony a perfect unity is achieved, and every element
is necessary in its place for the constitution of this unity. But
the ground of this necessity is in the whole, and at any given
moment in the development there is as yet no necessity. This
is an analogy of the eternal experience, the relation of eternity to history. Another form of the same analogy is the spectator at a play whose plot he knows. He watches every incident
in the light of its known consequences. The Greek tragedians
derived their irony from this situation. The process is essential,
because the meaning of the play cannot be extracted and expressed in a proposition. Furthermore, the movement of the

---

[1] *Nature, Man and God*, p. 447.
[2] Ibid., pp. 448, 479f.
[3] *Christ the Truth*, p. 107; *Nature, Man and God*, p. 441.

plot is free in the sense that the beginning does not determine the middle or the end. "The story of the drama is a self-determining system, where the parts are explained only by the whole which they constitute."[1]

A better version of this analogy is that of the dramatist in the act of writing a play. He does not know in advance what he is going to write; he apprehends his thought in the act of expressing it. In expressing the unfolding meaning in his own thoughts, he discovers the meaning. Dramatists, such as Shaw, claim that once they have launched their characters, they have no control over their conduct. Yet in another sense the dramatist is in complete control, because it is his own thought which is being articulated. His thought in self-expression is immanent in the play, yet he transcends the play which depends upon him for its existence. But since he fulfils his nature in writing, the play is of vital consequence to him.[2]

The analogy of the dramatist in the act of writing breaks down because his creation is not actually alive. It becomes necessary to conceive the characters as creating their own parts as the play proceeds. This leads to the analogy of the father training his children. The father is the source of his children's existence and the creative artist who works out his purpose through the living wills of his children. The course of their lives is of vital concern to him, but he exercises his control not through coercion but through love. This analogy breaks down because the father never has as full control as does the artist, and the father is also finite and subject to successiveness.[3]

Thus, it becomes necessary to combine the two analogies in the picture of a play being acted by the children of the

[1] *Christ the Truth*, p. 108; cf. pp. 224, 329; *Mens Creatrix*, pp. 357, 359f.
[2] *Mens Creatrix*, p. 360; *Christ the Truth*, p. 224; *Nature, Man and God*, pp. 441f.
[3] *Mens Creatrix*, p. 360; *Christ the Truth*, pp. 224f; *Nature, Man and God*, pp. 442f.

dramatist and composed by them as they act according to the characters of which their father is the source and which he knows so well as to be sure of the general course they will take. This is the closest analogy Temple can conceive to the relation of eternity to history.[1]

These analogies of the relation of eternity to history lead Temple to a differentiation in eternity or in the Godhead. God must control men through their apparent good, so he does not know beforehand exactly how they will respond to the various modes of his self-manifestation. In so far as he is immanent and active in the process, the precise mode of the future is unknown to him. Yet because he is transcendent and the process utterly depends on him, the future is known with absolute certainty.

> To Him the contingent is still contingent, as not being compelled by its own past; yet the whole is necessary, and therefore also all its parts; and the whole is the expression of His will. So He knows the contingent as contingent and yet knows it with certainty.[2]

Thus, we have God in eternity and God in time, God transcendent and God immanent, God of absolute knowledge and God of temporal experience.[3]

This, of course, is a philosophical statement of Temple's explicitly Christian view of the meaning of history. Although the entire course of cosmic history would afford a full revelation of the meaning of history, this meaning is also fully manifest in Christ. "What we see in Him is what we should see in the history of the universe if we could apprehend that history in its completeness."[4] But these two manifestations of the meaning of history are not separate and independent.

---

[1] *Christ the Truth*, p. 329; *Nature, Man and God*, p. 443.

[2] *Nature, Man and God*, p. 445.

[3] *Mens Creatrix*, p. 365; *Christ the Truth*, pp. 330f; *Nature, Man and God*, pp. 445f.

[4] *Mens Creatrix*, p. 318.

It is to be remembered that we have not the World-History without the Incarnation as one expression of the Divine Will and the Life of the Incarnate as another; for that Life is a part of History, though it reveals the principle of the whole, and it is through its occurrence in the midst of History that History is fashioned into an exposition of the principle there revealed.[1]

Various conditions of finding meaning in history have now been stated. The meaning of a process may lie in its result or in its course or in both. Since the successive as such cannot display meaning, the meaning of history cannot lie entirely in its course. Thus, it must lie partly in its result, and the end of history cannot be meaningless. But the meaning of history cannot lie entirely in its result. Therefore, its meaning must lie partly in its course, but this can be apprehended only from a point of view outside the process from which the whole course can be seen as a single whole. Thus, the meaning of history depends upon its being seen in the light of eternity. However, history cannot be epiphenomenal to eternity; it must be essential to eternity. History must have the ground of its existence and not just an explanation of its content in eternity. History must have meaning for eternity and not be simply an expression of eternity.

Temple's definition of the meaning of history is given in terms of his category of purpose. "History is the manifestation and working out of the eternal purpose." "History is the arena wherein the Divine Purpose is being fulfilled."[2] The goal of this purpose is defined in terms of Temple's value theory as the commonwealth of value.

> If our whole account of the nature of Value is true, or even only contains Truth, then the meaning of History is found in the development of an ever wider fellowship of ever richer personalities. The goal of History, in short, is the Commonwealth of Value.[3]

---

[1] *Mens Creatrix*, p. 318n.

[2] *Christ the Truth*, p. 226; *Christianity as an Interpretation of History*, p. 13; cf. pp. 15, 22; *Nature, Man and God*, pp. 432f; *Personal Religion and the Life of Fellowship*, p. 15.

[3] *Nature, Man and God*, p. 448; cf. p. 451.

This means the achievement of individual unity and universal fellowship, a loving society of free spirits. Put in more theological terms the goal of history is the Kingdom of God, the sovereignty of love, the redemption of the world.[1]

Temple affirms the reality of progress in history toward this goal, but he does not limit progress to the approach to a specific goal. History does not have to be finite in time to have meaning. Infinite progress is not a meaningless concept. "Progress may take the form of an ever wider application of a principle which sets no limit to its application, and then there is nothing self-contradictory in the idea of infinite progress."[2] The principle of love can be developed to an infinite extent through a multiplication of the persons between whom this relationship is established.[3]

In *Christ the Truth* Temple elaborates certain principles by which the actual course of history can be interpreted. The fulfilment of human destiny is in the achievement of two unities, the unity of individual personality and the unity of universal fellowship. The fundamental issue in history is the struggle between these two unities, which is the struggle between freedom and order. Little or no freedom was present in the primitive societies and the ancient empires. The quest for true freedom first appeared in Greece. The purpose to achieve political liberty follows a curve. As long as there is external danger or pressure, liberty can be maintained without breaking up the social unity. But when the external pressure is removed, the temptations to selfishness incident to liberty lead to internal disruptions until tyranny establishes order at the expense of liberty. This is illustrated in the history of Greece, Rome, and modern Europe.[4]

---

[1] *Christ the Truth*, pp. 91, 235, 238; *Personal Religion and the Life of Fellowship*, pp. 19ff, 23; *Christianity as an Interpretation of History*, pp. 8, 19.

[2] *Nature, Man and God*, p. 440.

[3] *Christianity as an Interpretation of History*, pp. 8f; cf. *Mens Creatrix*, pp. 272, 290; *Nature, Man and God*, p. 213.

[4] *Christ the Truth*, pp. 90-4.

On a deeper level human history is the working out of the Platonic principles of desire, pride, and reason in their interaction with each other. There are three primary relations in which one human being may stand to another: he may ignore him, compete with him, or co-operate with him. These relations are the life of desire, the life of pride, and the life of reason, and they pass from the character of the citizens to the ordering of the state. Each relation or principle has its necessary place in the social life of the state. As in the structure of reality itself, each level is the necessary foundation of the next above and is fulfilled in being possessed by it. The various impulses of desire will give rise to a minimal social order. This is the indispensable economic basis of every society, but it cannot exist in its purity. Pride will give rise to the society of social contract of Glauco and Hobbes, although this is never the actual history of the origin of any state. The growth of the dominion of reason can be traced in the internal and the external relations of a society. Reason produces concern for the social goods of knowledge, beauty, and fellowship, which tend to overcome the class war deriving from desire and pride. Reason also insists on the equality of the nations and the necessity of a community of nations. However, all the forces which tend to make for progress in history are based on self-interest, and the positive forces, such as disinterested love of parents, devotion to righteousness, and the fellowship in spiritual goods, give no promise of being able to overcome selfishness completely. "Man needs education; but still more he needs conversion. Man needs political progress and social reform; but still more he needs redemption; man needs peace and security, but still more he needs eternal life."[1]

It is also in *Christ the Truth* that Temple elaborates his explicitly Christian interpretation of history. The Christian revelation affects the interpretation of history in the first place in the scale of values. The eternal is more important than the

---

[1] *Christ the Truth*, p. 106; cf. pp. 94–106.

temporal. Fellowship with the eternal spirit and partnership in the eternal goods must be more important than any temporal interest. If history is the manifestation and working out of the eternal purpose, temporal success must depend upon conformity to the eternal mind and will. If the eternal mind and will are expressed in love, then all selfishness is self-defeating, and every purpose of love will be successful. Even in the animal world mutual aid rather than mere competition is the law of progress.[1]

But is eternal love manifested in a world in which accident can at any moment devastate man's hopes? An accident is a natural event of which the causes have no connection with the causes of the human conduct affected by it. It is an interference with human purposes due to natural forces which have no relation to the purpose interfered with. God is the cause of accidents only in the sense that he is the source of the world in which they occur. Thus, an accident is not a special act of divine volition but a particular illustration of the fact that all human purposes must be fulfilled in a world subject to general laws. And general laws are a necessary basis of moral life and purpose which is God's purpose for man. Furthermore, it is the experience of religious people that God occasionally intervenes to avoid accidents, but such interventions are rare and raise the question of why God does not always intervene. If the goal of human life is to acquire detachment from the temporal and to become rooted in the eternal, there is no influence more powerful in the education for this than accident. "'Accident', speaking broadly, is one of the most effective forces for the spiritualizing of men."[2]

The key principle in the Christian interpretation of history is the sovereignty of love which is manifested in judgement. This sovereignty is seen in the catastrophes resulting from

---

[1] *Christ the Truth*, pp. 225–9.
[2] Ibid., p. 235; cf. pp. 229–38.

reliance on principles at variance with it. The fall of Jerusalem
was due to the nationalistic ambition of the Jews which
caused them to reject Christ. Likewise the fall of the Roman
Empire, the break-up of medieval Europe, the French Revolution, and the First World War were catastrophes issuing
from the rejection of love and thus vindicating its sovereignty.
God's judgements are not primarily interventions but the
working out of the laws of cause and effect in the moral world
created by God.

> [A divine judgement] is the taking effect of a constant law upon
> those who have brought themselves under its operation. . . .
> When the calamity comes in accordance with the law there is no
> arbitrary intervention, but it is a Divine act. It is the working
> out of the Divine purpose, as expressed in the law which attaches
> calamity to selfish choices.[1]

This leads directly to the consideration of a last judgement,
the climax or fulfilment of history. Is the judgement in history
completed in a final judgement? Some judgements in history
are final, as, for example, when a nation is wiped out. Also an
individual may persist in rejecting love, and the persistence
may become final, so that "there is nothing left that Almighty
Love can do with such a soul except to bring it to an end".[2]
The question of the final judgement is the religious form of the
question as to whether time will have an end. There may be
no end of successive events, but there must be an end of human
history by terrestrial catastrophe or changing physical conditions. This end must be the full establishment of the
sovereignty of love, the Kingdom of God. The condition of
the coming of the Kingdom is that men should evaluate their
experience not as temporal only but as constitutive of eternity.

[1] *Christianity as an Interpretation of History*, pp. 14f; cf. *Christ the Truth*,
pp. 238–42, 247f; *Thoughts in War-Time*, p. 12.
[2] *Christ the Truth*, p. 249. This represents a modification of the universal-
ism implied in *Mens Creatrix*, p. 290, but this annihilationism is itself
modified in *Nature, Man and God*, pp. 414f.

However, the final consummation cannot be in history, because it must involve the universal fellowship of all generations. The Christian hope is not utopian. "History moves to a climax which is historical because it occurs in, and crowns, the course of History, but which is in its own nature a transition to a new order of experience."[1]

---

[1] *Nature, Man and God*, pp. 450f; cf. *Christ the Truth*, pp. 248–52; *Christianity as an Interpretation of History*, pp. 21f.

Part II

THE THEISTIC ARGUMENT

I I

THE FIRST DIALECTICAL
TRANSITION

TEMPLE intends his Gifford Lectures to be a study in natural
theology which he defines as a philosophical discipline which
investigates the true nature and general validity of religion,
sets it in the context of our knowledge of the universe, and
investigates its claim to be the dominant element in man's
experience exercising over all the rest a certain judgement
and control.[1] The quarter of the Lectures devoted to the
dialectical argument for theism is presumably an inquiry into
the general validity of religion or an investigation of its claim
to be the dominant element in man's experience.

Temple states in an introductory note that this argument
consists of four dialectical transitions. It has been suggested
that this procedure seems to be out of accord with his statement that the dialectical method cannot successfully be used
as a guide for the thinking of individual philosophers except
in the case of subjects which are highly abstract or extremely
limited in scope.[2] Since there is no explicit mention of a
dialectical method in the body of the argument, it may be
that the idea that his argument consisted of dialectical
transitions was an afterthought which was placed in the
introductory note. Another possibility is that the above statement about the applicability of the dialectical method refers
specifically to the method developed by Hegel, and that the
method of the theistic argument is dialectical only in the
general sense employed by Plato.

---

[1] *Nature, Man and God*, pp. 18, 28.   [2] Ibid., pp. 57f.

The first transition is from the picture of the world offered by science through the emergence of mind to immanent theism.[1] It consists of the convergence of arguments that only mind supplies a self-explanatory principle of origination and that mind is the principle of unity of any organism or process in which it occurs. The scientific picture of the world involving the emergence of mind and the development of apprehension and consciousness has been discussed in connection with its epistemological significance.[2] The universe as pictured by science might exist apart from any immanent or transcendent mind or spirit. But the emergence of mind in the world process leads to a reconsideration of the scientific picture of the process, because this emergence cannot be explained by the scientific picture. "All attempts to trace in evolution an explanation of the emergence of mind have totally failed."[3] Emergence means that the emergent entity is not to be accounted for in terms of the antecedent stages of the process nor by any known principle of teleology. Temple believes that it represents a certain agnosticism as well as a preference for continuity rather than radical discontinuity. Either the first term of the process or its totality will supply the ground for its various phases including mind. Temple holds that "either assumption will necessitate the inference from the mere fact of knowledge to a spiritual (or at least a 'mental') interpretation of existence".[4]

The emergence of mind must be due either to a combination of circumstances which are not conscious or mental, or to a new creative act of that which is the ground of all existence, or to its having been present throughout the process in a rudimentary and imperceptible form. Temple believes that the first possibility must be ruled out, because "to suppose that a combination of non-conscious physical functions can be the cause of consciousness in the organism concerned is to assert

---

[1] *Nature, Man and God*, pp. 129–34, 198–201, 212–20, 247, 256f, 312.
[2] See Chapter 5.   [3] *Nature, Man and God*, p. 132.
[4] Ibid., p. 130.

so great disparity between cause and effect as to rob the notion of causation of all meaning".[1] To hold that, when a certain stage of complexity is reached, consciousness always appears, is an occasionalism which evades the issue. "A philosophy which leaves the appearance of consciousness or mind as a brute fact incapable of explanation or of intelligible relation to the general scheme of things is self-condemned as bankrupt."[2]

Temple believes that no ultimate issue hangs on a choice between the second and third possibilities mentioned above, although the third is more compatible with the scientific preference for continuity, as is indicated in Whitehead's approach.[3] He also points out later that the second is not possible in the form described, for if there is such a creative ground of existence capable of intervening to intrude mind into the process, it is inconceivable that it should have no connection with the process except at that point. It must be presumed to have been active in or upon the process throughout its course.[4] What is required is an explanation of the emergence of mind, and this in the nature of the case will be an explanation of the whole process.

In our experience matter does not generate thought nor thought matter. Mind cannot be reduced to any combination of matter, and matter cannot be reduced to any activity of mind. We cannot argue from fact to value or from value to fact. The world process contains matter and mind, fact and value in a continuum in the form of a process.[5]

In the world of matter, however, there is no known principle which is self-explanatory. It is always possible to ask of any principle or system of experience, why is it so and not otherwise? Temple believes that the theory that every combination of the ultimate particles of matter will occur sometime in the process does not represent a sound logic of

---

[1] Ibid., pp. 198f.   [2] Ibid., p. 199.   [3] See Chapter 5.
[4] *Nature, Man and God*, pp. 212, 214.   [5] Ibid., pp. 130f, 217f.

probability. Furthermore, it is untenable in relation to an organic process which "exhibits a selected flux of participating forms. No reason, internal to history, can be assigned why that flux of forms, rather than another flux, should have been illustrated."[1]

Also, if we start with the lowest category or the less developed stage of the process, the appearance of mind and its value-oriented activities represents a breach of continuity which can be accounted for in terms of the lowest category only by considering it as an epiphenomenon which produces no modifications in the process. Temple claims that this explanation flouts the common experience of mankind and must be rejected. On this view value would be reduced to states of mind. But the common experience and judgement of value has as much claim to objectivity as any other, and doubt of this amounts to a scepticism which casts doubt upon the validity of the whole intellectual enterprise. Thus, beginning with matter or fact we cannot make sense of the fact of knowledge including the science which is the source of our original knowledge of matter.

The alternative method would be to take the fullest development of the process as the surest guide to the interpretation of the process as a whole. Mind is always aware of value in the process, "*universally in the form of Truth, commonly in the form of Beauty, sometimes in the form of Goodness*".[2] Since this means that mind discovers itself in the process, Temple concludes that mind is pervasive of reality. But since "where Mind is found, it is found as potentially, and always in some degree actually, the principle of unity of that through which it is active", it follows that "*Mind is the principle of unity in Reality, or at least the fullest expression of that principle known to us*".[3]

In the realm of mind and value, which is the highest

---

[1] Whitehead, *Process and Reality*, p. 64; quoted, *Nature, Man and God*, p. 131.

[2] *Nature, Man and God*, p. 219.   [3] Ibid., pp. 201, 219.

category or the fullest development of the process, there is a principle which is self-explanatory and requires no further explanation, namely, purpose or intelligent choice. "When in tracing any causal nexus we reach the activity of a will fulfilling a Purpose with which we sympathize, we are in fact satisfied",[1] because this alone combines efficient and final causation and here mind has referred the occurrence to itself as a cause. Mind determined by good as apprehended is an ultimate principle of explanation and a true principle of origination.[2]

The hypothesis suggested by this is that "Mind contains the explanation of the World-Process".[3] The result is that mind which appears late in the process must have been active from the beginning as an immanent principle. This Temple describes as "immanent theism".[4] This hypothesis includes the cause and origin of the world process as well as its governing principle, because purpose or will seeking an intelligible good is a principle of origination.[5] Temple concludes: "There exists, expressing itself in the universe, and most fully (within our knowledge) in man, a reality characterized by mind, and in some sense, by personality."[6]

Temple believes that the argument to a first cause can never be a satisfactory explanation of the world process, because there is the possibility of an infinite series, and the question is never answered, why this series and not another?[7] However, Temple considers his own argument to be modelled on Aristotle's argument to a first cause in the *Metaphysics* but

[1] "Some Implications of Theism", p. 418.
[2] *Nature, Man and God*, pp. 131f, 220, 256. For Temple's treatment of purpose in this connection, cf. *The Faith and Modern Thought*, pp. 16f; *The Nature of Personality*, p. xxiv; *The Kingdom of God*, p. 108; *Mens Creatrix*, p. 89; *Christ the Truth*, pp. 7f, 11; *Christian Faith and Life*, p. 13; *Christianity in Thought and Practice*, pp. 71–4; *Religious Experience*, p. 79.
[3] *Nature, Man and God*, p. 132.   [4] Ibid., p. 133.
[5] *Christ the Truth*, p. 8; *Mens Creatrix*, p. 89.
[6] *Nature, Man and God*, p. 247
[7] *The Faith and Modern Thought*, pp. 8, 15; *The Nature of Personality*, p. xxiv; "Some Implications of Theism", p. 418.

9

developed in terms of final causation rather than efficient causation. Aristotle gave the suggestion for this modification in his description of the Unmoved Mover as setting other things in motion as an object of desire.[1] Thus, when mind, moved by good as apprehended, initiates activity, no further explanation is needed.

As has been suggested in Chapter 8 the cogency of this argument is seriously affected by the confusion in Temple's use of the term "mind". This becomes especially clear in the first formulation of the argument:

> We find that the Process is akin to Mind, that Mind arises in the course of it, and that Mind does exhibit what is essentially the thing required—a self-explanatory principle of origination. It is then more reasonable to test the hypothesis that Mind contains the explanation of the World-Process than to refuse to test it.[2]

The mind that the process is akin to is human mind, because Temple states, "There is a kinship between Mind and the World, so that we can assert of the World a relation of correspondence to Mind as we know it in ourselves".[3] The mind which arises in the course of the process and which exhibits the self-explanatory principle of origination is clearly human mind.[4] Therefore, it may be assumed that the fourth use of "Mind" in the above passage also refers to human mind. But then the result of the argument would not be immanent theism but some kind of subjective idealism.[5] Apparently Temple intends the fourth use to mean mind in a generic sense including divine mind, but if the argument is to be consistent, this would require the first three uses to be the generic sense also. This is not possible, however, since the

---

[1] *Metaphysics*, L, 1072 b 3; referred to, "Some Implications of Theism", p. 418; *Nature, Man and God*, pp. 220n, 256f.

[2] *Nature, Man and God*, p. 132.   [3] Ibid., p. 130.

[4] Cf. ibid., pp. 120, 131f, 219f.

[5] Cf. F. R. Tennant, review of *Nature, Man and God*, *The Journal of Theological Studies*, XXXVI (July 1935), p. 314.

process is akin only to mind as we know it in ourselves. The expansion of this to refer to generic mind would require demonstration that what is true of human mind is also true of animal and divine mind or at least the latter. But such demonstration is impossible, because animal mind does not exhibit the self-explanatory principle of origination and divine mind does not arise in the process. Furthermore, it is apparent from the context of Temple's definition of the generic term mind that it does not include divine mind.[1]

However, a reconstruction of the argument of the above passage is possible if "Mind" in all four uses is taken in the sense of a principle or a "mode of being and activity",[2] which can refer to both human and divine mind. Such a mode of being and activity does arise in the process and exhibits the required self-explanatory principle of origination. And the hypothesis that such an immanent principle or mode of being and activity contains the explanation of the world process can be called immanent theism. This reconstruction can similarly be applied to the statements of the argument which occur later in the Gifford Lectures.[3]

Temple's commentators generally agree that he assumes too easily the unique explanatory value of the category of purpose when it is applied not only to certain kinds of activity within the world but also to the world as a whole.[4] In his earlier works proof of the explanatory power of purpose is given in the fact that it satisfies our minds. In his later works, however, the explanatory character of purpose is put forward heuristically, a hypothesis supported but not demonstrated by reason and experience. E. W. Edwards suggests that the explanatory power of the category of purpose is illusory since inexplicabilities are merely transferred from the term "world" to the phrase "purposer purposes" or "God".

---

[1] *Nature, Man and God*, p. 120.   [2] Ibid.

[3] Ibid., pp. 133f, 219f, 257.

[4] Cf. Edwards, loc. cit., p. 241; Tennant, loc. cit., p. 314; Stedman, loc. cit., pp. 303f; Emmet, "The Philosopher", op. cit., p. 527.

Another commentator claims that this transference is to a question of a different order and that an ultimate principle of explanation has been arrived at.[1]

It is not clear, however, how Temple's formulation differs finally from the first cause argument which he criticizes, how "purposer purposes" differs basically from "first cause causes". Temple criticizes the pictures of reality offered by Bradley and Whitehead in that they do not explain the existence of reality as a whole. Reality is pictured as a brute fact, and there is no reason why it exists or why it takes the form it does.[2] Temple's argument offers a possible answer to these questions, but does not avoid the possibility of their being asked at the next stage: why does God exist and have the purposes which he has? Furthermore, Temple does not deal with the criticism of the cosmological argument by Hume and Kant to the effect that the concept of causation is limited to the world of experience and cannot meaningfully be extended beyond it.

[1] Trueblood, op cit., pp. 147f.
[2] *The Kingdom of God*, pp. 107f; *Christ the Truth*, p. 10; *Nature, Man and God*, pp. 260, 263.

12

THE SECOND DIALECTICAL
TRANSITION

THE second transition is from immanent theism through a consideration of the experience of value and the relation of personality to process to transcendent theism.[1] In this transition Temple uses two converging lines of argument, each of which he considers sufficient to establish transcendent theism.

The first line of argument is a consideration of the ultimate implications of the higher levels of the experience of value. *"The mind recognizes in Truth, or in the Mind expressed in Truth, a proper object of reverence quite other than is appropriate as a part of the mind's apprehension of bare fact."*[2] Reverence for truth as august and compelling, as claiming allegiance and service, *"is only justifiable if the order of reality is the expression of a personal mind, for the sense of moral obligation towards Truth is of that quality which is only appropriate in connection with personal claims"*.[3] Temple realizes that this is not an argument but an intuitional judgement. He merely appeals to the fact that obligations arising from personal relationships have a special quality distinguishing them from and giving them priority over obligations deriving from impersonal relations and that the obligation toward truth has the former quality.[4]

Likewise the appreciation of beauty is unintelligible unless it involves *"communication from, and communion with, personal spirit"*.[5] In an earlier lecture Temple has stated that the

---

[1] *Nature, Man and God*, lecture x.   [2] Ibid., p. 249.
[3] Ibid., p. 250.   [4] Ibid., pp. 152f, 156, 190, 249–51.
[5] Ibid., p. 253.

testimony of aesthetic experience and the artistic consciousness "*is an unambiguous affirmation of transcendent Mind apprehended by reason of its immanence in Nature physical and spiritual*".[1]
He immediately adds that justification of the term "transcendent" will come later (in the second transition) but that
already it is unavoidable. The mental attitude in the deep
appreciation of beauty is akin to worship.[2]

The same conclusion is involved in moral goodness. The
essence of morality is personal communion or respect for persons. The duty to obey conscience or the moral law makes the
kind of claim which can be made only by persons. Failure in
duty is felt not only as injury to the neighbour, degradation of
the self, and breach of the moral law, but also as the flouting
of that which justly claims our reverence. "*For no Law,
apart from a Lawgiver, is a proper object of reverence. . . . The
reverence of persons can be appropriately given only to that which is
itself at least personal.*"[3] In conclusion, Temple states that
to doubt the intimations of these feelings is to adopt a
"scepticism of the instrument" such as to make all conviction
impossible.[4]

Temple describes the second part of this transition as a
converging line of argument which leads to the same result.
However, it appears to be also a completion of the first part.
In the first part he argues that the experience of value in its
various forms indicates the personal nature of the ground of
the universe. In a previous lecture, as we have noted, he has
stated that the experience of value implies the transcendent
character of the ground of the universe,[5] but that apparently
is not his purpose in the first part of the second transition.
Thus, the first part of the argument in lecture x requires the
further proof that person is always transcendent, and this is
carried out in the second part of this transition.

After reviewing the first transition Temple asks if the mind

[1] *Nature, Man and God*, p. 161.   [2] Ibid., pp. 156f, 190.
[3] Ibid., p. 254.   [4] Ibid., pp. 190f, 254f.
[5] Ibid., p. 161.

which pervades, sustains, and directs the world process has its
whole being in it or is something over and above the process.
Temple begins with a criticism of the theology of Whitehead,
with whom he has been in general agreement up to this
point. On the basis of his philosophy of organism Whitehead
claims to give an explanation of the world process in terms of
the "primordial nature of God". God is also the source of
"relevant novelty" and the "principle of concretion" in the
process.[1] Temple claims that this is only a verbal solution
of the problem of explaining the process. He points out that
this is supplemented at the end of *Process and Reality* with the
concept of the "consequent nature of God". But Temple
believes that Whitehead is not justified on the basis of his
philosophy of organism in describing God as he does here.
Whitehead speaks of "the perfection of God's subjective aim"
and describes God as "the great companion—the fellow-
sufferer who understands" and as "the poet of the world,
with tender patience leading it by his vision of truth, beauty
and goodness".[2] These images imply personality in the Godhead, and Temple suggests that Whitehead's concepts of
"creativity", the "primordial nature", and the "consequent
nature" would be made more coherent if described in the
personal concepts of classical trinitarian theology. But Whitehead would have to reject these concepts, because they involve personality and thus transcend his final category of
organism.

Temple concludes that, although Whitehead claims not to
transcend the category of organism, he has introduced images
and terminology which properly belong to the category of
personality. This perhaps accounts for the confusion among
commentators on Whitehead in regard to his attribution of
personality to God. Hartshorne believes that Whitehead

[1] *Process and Reality*, pp. 64, 229, 345; referred to, *Nature, Man and God*,
p. 258.
[2] *Process and Reality*, pp. 489f, 497; quoted, *Nature, Man and God*, pp.
259f.

attributes full personality to God.[1] On the other hand, D. Emmet, author of *Whitehead's Philosophy of Organism*, holds that "Whitehead leads us finally to the conception of a logical-aesthetic order, and Temple is, I think, justified in his criticism that much of the quasi-personalist language which Whitehead uses about this at the end of his *Process and Reality* goes beyond what is warranted by his own theory."[2]

Temple concludes that, although Whitehead introduces terminology concerning God which belongs properly to personality, he apparently stops at the category of organism. Thus, he presents God and the world as completely correlated to each other.[3] Because they are completely correlated and each is explained by the other, the totality of God plus world is not explained. Temple suggests that an explanation is possible only if we pass

> beyond Organism to Personality—beyond the notion of inner unification by coordination of function to the notion of self-determination by reference to apprehended good. *But Personality is always transcendent in relation to Process.*[4]

Temple distinguishes three levels of action or reaction: mechanical, organic, and purposive or personal. Organic reaction differs from mechanical reaction in that the reaction is determined by the whole organism as a unity. It is the condition of the organism at the moment which determines the reaction. Purposive or personal action, however, is determined not only by the whole being of the agent at the moment of action but also by an aspiration to become what it is not, by an ideal of itself. The apprehension of what may be exercises efficient causation over the personal agent in his choice of

---

[1] "Whitehead's Idea of God", *The Philosophy of Alfred North Whitehead*, Paul Arthur Schilpp (ed.) (Evanston: Northwestern University, 1941), pp. 548f.

[2] "The Philosopher", op. cit., p. 528.

[3] Cf. *Process and Reality*, p. 429; referred to, *Nature, Man and God*, p. 260.

[4] *Nature, Man and God*, pp. 260f.

conduct. The future is a real factor in decision as it is not in the case of organic reaction. "What we have called the freedom of mind, with the kind of self-determination that results from it, implies also self-transcendence, and therefore a self that transcends."[1]

Temple considers the principle of personality as the most adequate for explaining the world process. It accounts for the appearance of self-determining persons as episodes in the process. It supplies a ground of explanation which calls for no further explanation. It employs the highest known category for the explanation of the world, thus avoiding the necessity of explaining any existent by a principle lower in the scale of being than itself. Since it is a principle of which the characteristic is action with a view to future fruition, it combines efficient causation with rational coherence, because purposive actions cohere in an intelligible scheme.

Furthermore, since personality exhibits itself supremely in purposes of fellowship or love,[2] it needs for its full self-expression the existence of other persons. Thus, if the ultimate principle is personality whose purpose is love, then the occurrence of persons within the process is explained. Finally, this hypothesis "points to the reality of a Being of such nature as to disclose His character in specific acts, which revealing acts might supply evidence to set against the apparent evidence of ordinary experience".[3] Temple concludes: "*Our argument has led us provisionally at least, to the conclusion that the explanation of the world is to be sought in a Personal Reality, or to use the historic phrase, in a Living God.*"[4]

At this point it becomes clear that Temple's criticism of Whitehead might with equal force be applied to the conclusion of Temple's first transition. Either purposive mind cannot be completely immanent and then Temple has not arrived at immanent theism, or it is completely correlated with

---

[1] Ibid., p. 262.
[2] Ibid., lecture vii.
[3] Ibid., pp. 263f.
[4] Ibid., p. 265.

the world and therefore cannot be an ultimate explanation of the world. Clearly the conclusion of the first transition must either involve the second transition already or else it cannot be an explanation of the world. In order that mind be considered an ultimate principle for the explanation and origination of the world, it must be purposive and determined by good. But if it is purposive and determined by good, it must be personal and therefore transcendent. In brief, if mind is an explanation of the universe, it must be transcendent. If it is immanent, it cannot be such an explanation. However, this does not invalidate the first transition; the second transition merely draws out a conclusion necessarily implied in the first.

13

THE THIRD DIALECTICAL TRANSITION

THE first two transitions lead to a fully developed doctrine of theism, the theory that the explanation and ground of the world process is an immanent and transcendent personal God. The third and fourth transitions deal with problems of the relation between human beings and God, between finite minds and the transcendent mind, and thus are not strictly necessary to the argument for theism. They are elaborations of the meaning and significance of theism for mankind.

The third transition deals with the "Evil attendant upon finite minds and the resultant conception of the relation between these and the Transcendent Mind".[1] The transition is from the original dependence of finite minds upon the transcendent mind through the problem of evil to the soteriological dependence of finite minds upon the transcendent mind.

Temple begins this transition with a consideration of the source and nature of moral evil. He is satisfied that in subhuman nature there is a balance of good over evil and therefore no obstacle to a reasonable theism. The problem becomes serious at the human stage. The human mind by means of its capacity of imagination can offer to desire the stimulus which the appropriate physical objects offer to physical appetite. This results in a great expansion of the life of desire which may take the form of aspiration or of lust. Whether this expansion leads

---

[1] *Nature, Man and God*, p. xi; see lectures xiv, xv.

to evil or the higher ranges of human life depends upon the direction of attention which is determined by the mind. To desire evil for its own sake is impossible. The wrong direction of attention is due to the fact that what appears good to a particular mind may not be the real good. The condition of a man's mind or his character determines his apparent good, and his apparent good determines his conduct. "*Hence [the self] has—or rather is—the freedom which is perfect bondage. It is free, for the origin of its actions is itself: it is bound, for from itself there is no escape.*"[1]

It is because the human mind is finite that its apparent good may be different from the real good. It can distinguish good and evil, but because of its finitude, it cannot know the full significance of the goods it apprehends, and it cannot apprehend all goods. Its well-being depends upon God, but this fact falls beyond its apprehension.

> There is no inherent and absolute necessity for [the apparent good] to be other than the real good; yet the probability of divergence is so great as to amount to certainty for all practical purposes. . . . *The mind by a necessary tendency of its own nature attaches more importance to values which find their actualization in itself than to those which find their actualization elsewhere. . . . So [each man] becomes not only the subject of his own value judgements, which he can never cease to be, but also the centre and criterion of his own system of values which he is quite unfit to be.*[2]

In self-consciousness self-centredness becomes self-assertion. Although the general good is recognized as real, it is relatively powerless compared with the good-for-self.

> It is not utterly necessary that this should be so. . . . But that it should be so was "too probable not to happen". . . . Human sin was not a necessary episode in the divine plan; but it was always so closely implicated in the divine plan that it must be held to fall within the divine purpose.[3]

---

[1] *Nature, Man and God*, p. 385.   [2] Ibid., p. 365.
[3] Ibid., p. 366; cf. p. 501.

Since men are reciprocally determining beings, self-assertion in one person will cause a similar reaction in others by suggestion and in self-defence. The centre of trouble is the spirit or personality as a whole in action which is the will. The will is perverted, directed to the wrong end. The will aims at the wrong ends, because they have a stronger appeal to the personality as a whole. Yet finitude or selfhood is not evil, since it is the necessary condition of value and therefore of the highest good.

The response to truth, beauty, and goodness affords a partial escape from bondage to the self, because the apprehension of these inherent values "involves a submission of all that is special or particular in the self to the impress of the object".[1] Temple believes that such response is to the divine initiative as the ground of value in the creation. Truth and beauty may effect a deliverance in certain areas of life, but goodness can effect a deliverance capable of being complete in range if not in type. The distinctive sphere of goodness is that of personal relationships, and the two ways in which the self is progressively delivered from self-centredness in this realm are disinterested love and widening of the area of loyalty and obligations. Disinterested love, however, is always limited in scope and is always called forth by some affinity with the self. No matter how greatly the circle of obligation is expanded, the self remains at the centre. Such deliverance is always partial; the goal cannot be reached by continuous progress.

Neither man nor society can attain to perfection in this way but only by the total elimination of self-centredness. A sharp break is necessary which in the language of religion is called conversion or new birth.

> What is quite certain is that the self cannot by any effort of its own lift itself off its own self as centre and resystematize itself about God as its centre. Such radical conversion must be the act of God. . . . Nothing can suffice but a redemptive act.[2]

---

[1] Ibid., p. 385.   [2] Ibid., p. 397.

This redemptive act must be a manifestation of the spirit of the whole such that it will cause the self to submit willingly to removal from self-centredness to God-centredness. The only kind of act which can effect this is an act of sacrificial love. "*The one hope, then, of bringing human selves into right relationship to God is that God should declare His love in an act, or acts, of sheer self-sacrifice, thereby winning the freely offered love of the finite selves which He has created.*"[1]

This raises the problem of the spiritual freedom of the finite spirit in relation to the infinite spirit. Temple struggles valiantly with this traditional problem of theology. First, he states that this freedom lies in the response to the divine initiative. The nature of this response is determined by the nature of the self, and this is not wholly determined by past history or present environment. "Every self is in part an original contribution to the scheme of reality and is moreover, in the very act of giving or refusing its response, a self-determining system of experience."[2] No one can be saved against his will. If God exercised compulsion over the will, this would not be a free response, and the will would remain outside his spiritual control.

Yet if this were the final answer, it would make man the master of his fate over against God. And the witness of profound religious experience is that the response is a divine gift. So Temple finally concludes by ascribing everything to God. "*All is of God: the only thing of my very own which I can contribute to my own redemption is the sin from which I need to be redeemed. . . . We are clay in the hands of the Potter, and our welfare is to know it.*"[3] This seems to amount to a divine determinism or predestination. Although Temple states that such a doctrine is untenable, he believes that some form of the doctrine of election is unavoidable.

In this transition Temple is attempting to describe the

---

[1] *Nature, Man and God*, p. 400.   [2] Ibid., p. 399.
[3] Ibid., pp. 401f.

relation between finite minds and the infinite mind, between man and God, in such a way that neither God nor finitude nor selfhood is the source of evil. He holds that there is no obstacle to theism in sub-human nature, because there is a balance of good over evil there. He admits, however, that there is already a problem in the existence of any evil at all, and he deals with this in the fourth transition.

Temple's analysis of evil at the human level is rather confused. He is not clear as to whether it is finitude or the condition of the mind which causes the apparent good to differ from the true good.[1] He is not clear as to whether it is finitude or a "necessary tendency of its own nature" which causes the mind to attach more importance to values which find their actualization in itself than to those which find it elsewhere.[2] He is not clear as to whether the mind knows the true good and rejects it because of its bias toward evil or does not know it because of finitude.[3]

Although he attempts to avoid this conclusion, his argument really points to finitude as the source of human evil. And although he denies it, this attributes the source of evil to the creator. The distinction is not clear when he states that sin falls within the "divine purpose" but God does not "will" it and it is not a necessary episode in the "divine plan". The probability that man would sin is "so great as to be distinguishable only in thought from certainty", but "there is, for God's *eternal* knowledge, no such thing as probability". This would seem to imply that God willed and planned that man should sin, but Temple concludes: "Yet that distinction in thought is important. For it means that God did not directly cause any man to sin."[4] This conclusion seems unjustified by the argument.[5] However, it is not Temple's main purpose here to give a complete theodicy, but only to indicate the soteriological dependence of finite minds upon the transcendent

[1] Cf. ibid., pp. 362, 365.   [2] Cf. ibid., pp. 365, 370.
[3] Cf. ibid., pp. 365f, 368.   [4] Ibid., pp. 366, 369; cp. p. 501.
[5] Cf. Matthews, op cit., pp. 18f.

mind. In elaborating the nature of this dependence he arrives at a paradox and is unable to resolve it. It is not clear whether the self makes any contribution by way of response to its own salvation or whether all is of God. At the end of the argument Temple seems to decide for the latter, but he does not explain how this can be reconciled with human freedom.[1]

[1] Cf. Tennant, loc. cit., p. 315; Edwards, loc. cit., pp. 241f.

14

THE FOURTH DIALECTICAL
TRANSITION

THE fourth and last transition[1] seems merely to draw out a
conclusion already implied in the third. "Natural Theology
culminates in a demand for the specific Revelation which its
principles forbid it to include in its own province."[2] This
transition is from the soteriological dependence of finite
minds upon the transcendent mind through the problem of
evil to the necessity of an actual justification of evil rather
than a merely possible justification.

Temple surveys the whole argument, reviews his analysis
of the problem of evil on the animal and human levels, and
reiterates the hopelessness of the human situation apart from
a divine act of revelation and redemption. The whole argument hangs on the solution of the problem of evil.

> The whole theistic scheme is condemned unless it can provide
> from its own principles, or at least in accordance with them, a
> solution in outline of the problem of evil. . . . What is wanted is
> some ground for belief that the occurrence of the evil is an
> actual element in the total good.[3]

He quotes approvingly Bosanquet's statement of this principle
in the first series of his Gifford Lectures,[4] but he points out
that in order to prove this it is necessary to show that the

---

[1] *Nature, Man and God*, lecture xx.   [2] Ibid., p. xii.
[3] Ibid., pp. 507f.
[4] *The Principle of Individuality and Value*, pp. 243ff, 254; quoted, *Nature,
Man and God*, pp. 508f.

various types of evil can be subordinated to the good in such a way as to contribute to its perfection. Temple examines suffering and sin and concludes that if they are overcome by fortitude and sacrificial love, respectively, the result is better than the absence of both. Significantly enough, although he lists error as one of the three forms of evil, he does not examine the question of that error which is not the result of sin. Apparently this is an irredeemable result of finitude. However, the possibility of such a justification of evil is not sufficient.

> But to show that evil is capable of justification is not to show that it is justified; and nothing less than this is required. If evil were only a possibility, a possible justification might suffice. But evil is actual, and only an actual justification is relevant.[1]

There is progress toward such a justification in the appreciation of value, because it involves a steadily decreasing detachment from self-centredness.

> At every point therefore the aspiration towards these forms of good requires a denial of self, and in the measure of its attainment passes over into worship, of which the meaning is total self-giving and self-submission to the Object of worship. This then, it seems, is man's true good—to worship.[2]

But the philosophy of religion or natural theology, as Temple calls it, cannot bring about this worship, this deliverance from bondage to the self. Natural theology can give assurance that there is a God who deserves worship and that such worship is the only way of deliverance from evil. But what is necessary is a confrontation by this God so that the supreme good may become the apparent good for every man. This means that the supreme good must display itself as "utterly selfless love", and in order to appeal to humans, it must be in the form of human personality, " a finite self whose apparent good is the real good".[3] Natural theology knows what is

---

[1] *Nature, Man and God*, p. 511.   [2] Ibid., p. 518.
[3] Ibid., p. 520.

required but cannot supply it. Natural theology ends with a hunger for divine revelation.

In the preface Temple states that his purpose "has not been to construct, stage by stage, a philosophical fabric where each conclusion becomes the basis of the next advance", but rather "to provide a coherent articulation of an experience which has found some measure of co-ordination through adherence to certain principles".[1] However, three pages later in the introductory note he speaks of the "stages of the argument" in terms of the four "dialectical transitions", and the course of the argument is clearly one in which each conclusion becomes the basis of the next advance.

The argument begins with the picture of the world offered by science and moves in turn through immanent theism, transcendent theism, the soteriological dependence of finite minds upon God, to the necessity of a special revelation for the solution of the problem of evil. As has been noted above, the first two transitions constitute the argument for theism. It is clear that this argument is a form of the cosmological argument in that it moves from specific characteristics of the world to the existence of a highest being. It also includes elements of what is traditionally referred to as the teleological argument for the existence of God.[2] It is cosmological in that it is modelled, as Temple states, on Aristotle's argument to a first cause. It is teleological in that the emergence of mind is an element of finite meaning which leads to the necessity of a bearer of infinite meaning or an infinite mind.

Tillich believes that this method of arguing from the world to God contradicts the idea of God, since God is discovered or inferred as a missing part of the world. He concludes that the arguments for the existence of God are expressions of the question of God which is implied in finitude. The idea of a first cause, a necessary substance, or an infinite meaning is a

[1] Ibid., p. viii.
[2] Tillich holds that the teleological argument is a species of the cosmological argument. See his *Systematic Theology*, I, pp. 208ff.

"hypostatized question". As questions they are true; as arguments, false. And this is the function of natural theology, according to Tillich, to elaborate the question of God.[1]

Casserley suggests a similar interpretation of the cosmological argument. If the term or concept which specifies the relationship between God and the world in such an argument is employed univocally, the argument is not valid and is not demonstrative. If, however, the argument is understood to be analogical rather than demonstrative and the term connecting God and the world is understood to be analogical rather than univocal, then the argument can be rightly held to show how belief in God helps to interpret the particular aspect of the world which is being considered.[2] Temple's formulation of the cosmological argument is open to this criticism, because he fails to make it clear that he is not using the term "mind" univocally.

In general such arguments are rational forms of Christian faith in God as creator.[3] The content of the knowledge secured by these arguments may be something quite different from the content of the knowledge secured by faith in the Christian revelation. The arguments will usually lead to deism or pantheism unless informed at every stage by faith in the Christian revelation.[4] That Temple became aware of this limitation of his argument is indicated by a statement he made some ten years later:

> The kind of deity established (if any is at all) by the various "proofs"—ontological, cosmological, and the like—is

[1] Tillich, *Systematic Theology*, I, pp. 205f, 209.

[2] Casserley, op cit., pp. 82ff.

[3] Cf. Erich Frank, *Philosophical Understanding and Religious Truth* (New York: Oxford University Press, 1945), p. 29; Austin Farrer, *Finite and Infinite* (Westminster: Dacre Press, 1943).

[4] Cf. Emil Brunner, *Revelation and Reason: The Christian Doctrine of Faith and Knowledge*, trans. Olive Wyon (Philadelphia: The Westminster Press, 1946), pp. 343, 347.

completely insufficient; it is usually little else than the rationality of the world presupposed in all argument about the world.[1]

The actual form of Temple's argument is the suggestion of a hypothesis which seems likely to explain the facts at hand and the testing of this hypothesis. However, the testing is carried out only implicitly, and actually in every case the suggested hypothesis is assumed in all later stages of the argument. For example, in lecture v Temple states:

> It is then more reasonable to test the hypothesis that Mind contains the explanation of the World-Process than to refuse to test it. That is not an extravagant claim. The whole future course of these lectures will be concerned with one very limited attempt to test that hypothesis and to develop its implications.[2]

Yet on the next page he states that the argument so far "has led—not to Naturalism—but to a fresh perception that if Nature (containing Mind) is to be explained at all, it is Mind that can alone supply the explanation". And in lecture viii he states dogmatically: "Mind is only explicable in itself, if it is the explanation of all else beside itself."[3] In other words, although Temple tries to give the impression of testing a hypothesis, his Gifford Lectures are really Christian apologetics, an exposition and defence of those of his Christian convictions which he considers to be within the area of natural theology. The lectures constitute a picture of what the world looks like when seen through the eyes of Christian faith. They are based ultimately on the suppressed premise of the truth of the Christian revelation.[4] This problem will be dealt with more fully in Part III.

---

[1] "What Christians Stand For in the Secular World", p. 3; cf. *Religious Experience*, p. 61.
[2] *Nature, Man and God*, p. 132. [3] Ibid., p. 213.
[4] Cf. Matthews, op cit., p. 11; Tennant, loc. cit., p. 316; Stedman, loc. cit., pp. 303f; K. E. Kirk, review of *Nature, Man and God*, *Church Quarterly Review*, CXX (July 1935), p. 307; J. S. Boys Smith, "A New Apologetic", *The Modern Churchman*, XXV (April 1935), p. 12f; Edwards, loc. cit., p. 240.

Part III

APPRAISAL AND RECONSTRUCTION

15

TEMPLE'S VIEW OF THE PHILOSOPHY OF RELIGION

OUR purpose has been to examine and assess William Temple's venture in the philosophy of religion broadly interpreted. The basic concepts of his religious philosophy have been examined and criticized, and the argument of his philosophy of religion or natural theology has been analysed. We are now in a position to appraise Temple's venture as a whole. The first problem is the assessment of Temple's interpretation of the philosophy of religion or natural theology in the Gifford Lectures. The second and larger question concerns the nature of Temple's religious philosophy, whether it is philosophy or theology, and how these two disciplines are related. This will involve a suggested redefinition of the philosophy of religion.

Temple defines the philosophy of religion as a philosophical discipline, by which he means that it is a department of philosophy. It is scientific in method and approach. Its aim is to investigate the true nature and general validity of religion by examining the actual religions of mankind. It should criticize religion and set religion as a whole in the context of our general knowledge of the universe. The philosopher of religion should know religion from the inside, that is, by participation as a worshipper, but as a philosopher he should not accept doctrines on authority.[1]

First of all, there is a confusing variety of terminology in Temple's definition of the philosophy of religion or natural

[1] *Nature, Man and God*, pp. 4, 7, 11, 17f, 26ff, 35, 42, 496.

theology. In the first two Gifford Lectures he uses the phrases "Natural Theology", "Natural Religion", and "Philosophy of Religion" almost interchangeably, but in the later lectures he uses "Natural Theology" exclusively. These terms are closely associated with "Philosophy", "Science", "Scientific Philosophy", and "Critical Philosophy", and they are set over against certain other terms: "Theology", "Religion", "Theological Philosophy", "Revealed Religion", and "Revealed Theology". Temple is apparently attempting to distinguish between (1) religion or revealed religion and its systematic formulation in theology or theological philosophy, and (2) the scientific and philosophical investigation of (1) in what he calls "Natural Theology", "Natural Religion", or "Philosophy of Religion". (The only obvious confusion of this distinction is where Temple defines theology as the science of religion, but he apparently means that theology is scientific in its own proper way although not in the same way as philosophy.) [1]

Although Temple states that the philosophy of religion should be scientific in method and approach, he also emphasizes the requirement that the philosopher of religion must know religion, his subject-matter, from the inside by personal experience as a worshipper. [2] This is probably the reason why there is some confusion in Temple's thought over the question of whether the validity of religion should be investigated or assumed in the philosophy of religion. On the one hand he states that it is very reasonable to accept religion as non-illusory at the outset and that the method of the philosophy of religion ideally requires that the validity of religion be assumed. But on the other hand he holds that one of the main functions of the philosopher of religion is to investigate the validity of religion, to investigate the claim of religion to be the dominant element of man's experience exercising over the rest of it a certain judgement and control, to distinguish true

----

[1] *Nature, Man and God*, pp. 44n, 45.   [2] Ibid., pp. 17, 27, 35, 496.

from false developments of the central principle of religion, and thus to include or exclude religion from his ultimate construction.[1]

But is it possible for a worshipping believer to come to a negative judgement as to the validity of his religion? It would seem that if he were to come to such a judgement, he would thereby cease to be a worshipping believer. It is possible, however, for him to subject his religion to radical scrutiny, criticism, and purgation and still remain a believer by means of what Temple describes as alternation of interest.

This leads to the question of what Temple means by the investigation of the general validity of "Religion" or "Religion as a whole".[2] By validity he apparently means truth. But is it possible to establish the truth of "Religion as a whole"? It would seem that the establishment of the general validity or truth of the Buddhist or Hindu world view would necessarily involve the establishment of the general invalidity or falsity of the Judeo-Christian world view and vice versa. By "Religion" Temple probably means theism, but the establishment of the validity of theism would certainly involve the establishment of the invalidity of non-theistic and polytheistic religions. Furthermore, it is certainly not possible to have a knowledge of "Religion as a whole" from within. If a person knows Mohammedanism from within as a worshipper, he necessarily cannot know Christianity in the same way, at least at the same time. It may be that Temple has in mind Schleiermacher's concept of the "essence of religion" or the "religion within the religions", but he does not make this clear.

The Gifford Lectures are intended to deal with the philosophy of religion so defined. To what extent has Temple carried out the programme described above?

Temple's method and approach are broadly philosophical and scientific in character. He begins with the picture of the

[1] Ibid., pp. 7f, 11, 18, 26ff, 35, 51.   [2] Ibid., p. 28.

world offered by science and inquires what is implied by this picture. He examines the date of science, art, and morality, as well as religion, in order to set religion in the context of our general knowledge of the universe. It is clear that Temple knows his subject-matter from the inside by participation as a worshipper. He investigates the validity of one aspect of religion, namely, theism, but he seems to do very little in the way of examining the nature of religion in general.

Furthermore, Temple carries out his programme with very little examination of the actual religions of mankind.[1] To be sure there is a considerable number of references to Christianity but only a very few and scattered references to any other religions. In the last lecture of the first series Temple states that up to this point he has confined his attention to forms of experience other than that of religion and that he now proposes to approach the question of transcendence without reference to religious experience.[2] The lectures of the second series contain more specific references to religious experience within the Christian tradition, but in the next to the last lecture Temple states: "Consequently we reach, from the consideration of the world as apprehended, and *without any reference to the data of distinctive religious experience*, the scheme familiar in the religious interpretation of the world."[3] Thus, it becomes clear that even Christianity is referred to only for purposes of illustration rather than as a central object of investigation.

Finally, although Temple clearly avoids the explicit acceptance of religious doctrines on the basis of authority, the whole of the Gifford Lectures actually amounts to Christian apologetics if not a direct statement of Christian doctrine. By means of the philosophy of religion which he has described as a scientific philosophical discipline Temple is able to arrive at the following conclusions: the existence of the

---

[1] See, however, the material referred to in Chapter 9.
[2] *Nature, Man and God*, p. 246.   [3] Ibid., p. 492, italics added.

transcendent and immanent personal creator-God of the Judeo-Christian tradition, Jesus' Summary of the Law as the only satisfactory form of the moral law, the expectation of divine acts of revelation, the marks of a true revelation, and the nature of the future life. He is also able to conclude that the fullness of revelation must be in the form of a personal life and must be an incarnation and not merely a theophany, that the deliverance of human life from involvement in sin can be accomplished only by a divine redemptive act, a declaration of God's love in an act of sheer self-sacrifice.[1] Apparently the only thing which the philosophy of religion cannot determine is whether and where this redemptive act has taken place.

In the Gifford Lectures Temple attempts to do something for which he was temperamentally unfitted. He proposes as his method a scientific examination of the facts of religion and the development of a theory to explain them. But he was a man of profound Christian faith, and what he actually has done is to arrange the facts so that they give support to his faith. The terms of the Gifford Trust and his proposed method hampered him in the carrying out of what he describes in the preface as an endeavour "to provide a coherent articulation of an experience which has found some measure of co-ordination through adherence to certain principles".[2] He was not able to hold consistently to the method of critical philosophy as he distinguished it from that of theological philosophy. There is some investigation of facts and argument, but this is employed to elaborate and support a vision of reality already present. The Gifford Lectures are really the articulation of a system of personal convictions and are based on the suppressed premise of the truth of the Christian faith.[3]

A letter from Professor Emil Brunner which was found in Temple's own copy of the Gifford Lectures expresses Brunner's

---

[1] Ibid., pp. 195, 264f, 322, 397, 400, 471f, 514.   [2] Ibid., p. viii.
[3] Cf. Emmet, "The Philosopher", op. cit., p. 531; see note 4, p. 139, chapter 14.

misgivings and confusion over what Temple is attempting to do in them. Brunner points out that in the first instance Temple's conception of natural theology or the philosophy of religion seems to be a truly philosophical and scientific discipline in which the power of logical argument is applied to the facts. In the second instance Temple's conception of the philosophy of religion seems to approach a Christian philosophy in which Christian faith is the starting point and the regulative principle. But Brunner points out that finally all of Temple's conclusions are determined by his Christian faith and the later lectures are "substantially, even predominantly, nothing more or less than Christian dogmatics, even though the difference in method is repeatedly stressed".[1]

The basic source of this confusion of purpose in the Gifford Lectures and of the discrepancy between Temple's stated aim and his at least partial failure to carry it out is what seems to be an overstatement of the contrast of temper and method between philosophy and theology or the philosophy of religion and theological philosophy. Temple believes that their respective attitudes of approach and general methods are diametrically opposed. Philosophy (and therefore the philosophy of religion) begins with the detailed experience of the various departmental sciences and attempts to take the principles of every department up into a coherent synthesis. Theological philosophy begins with the deliverances of religious experience as formulated by theology and seeks to offer explanations of the facts of experience by reference to the character of the supreme spirit. Philosophy tries to account for everything by the lowest category possible, whereas theology tries to do the same with the highest category of all. The temper of theology is one of assurance, while that of philosophy is inquiry.[2] So Temple asks, how can a religious

[1] Translated and quoted by Emmet, "The Philosopher", op. cit., pp. 531f.
[2] *Nature, Man and God*, pp. 30f, 35, 44f.

person be a philosopher, or how can a philosopher participate in a religion?

Temple's solution of this problem, as we have seen, is a deliberate alternation of interest and attention on the part of the philosopher of religion who is a believer. This is undoubtedly an illuminating and sound suggestion for the believing philosopher, but it implies that the philosopher who does not participate in a religion does not face this problem. This would seem to involve a fundamental misunderstanding of the essential character of philosophy. It will be the purpose of the final chapter to investigate this point and its implications for the philosophy of religion.

16

RELIGION, PHILOSOPHY, AND THEOLOGY

In order to clarify the essential character of philosophy it will be necessary to investigate the relation of religion and philosophy using an approach different from that of Temple. For this purpose it will be helpful to follow a suggestion made by Paul Tillich, among others, as to the nature of religion.[1] This suggestion follows from the fact that a human personality, looked at from one point of view, is made up of a cluster of interests, values, and concerns. Human life necessarily involves decisions to forgo certain concerns in favour of others. Thus, in the nature of the case there will be an ultimate concern for each person, namely, that value, interest, or concern which has top priority in the hierarchy or structure of concerns, that concern which always wins out when it comes into conflict with any other concern, that concern to which all others are sacrificed in a crisis. Then, following Tillich, religion can be defined as an attitude of loyalty or allegiance to such an ultimate concern.[2] This ultimate concern tends to pervade all of a person's life, to order and organize all the relative concerns, interests, and values into some kind of hierarchy, and thus to give meaning to all areas of life and experience.

[1] Here I am indebted to John A. Hutchison and James Alfred Martin, Jr, *Ways of Faith: An Introduction to Religion* (New York: The Ronald Press, 1953), ch. i; and Hutchison, op. cit., pp. 24ff.

[2] *The Protestant Era* (Chicago: The University of Chicago Press, 1948), pp. xv, 59. This concept is found in slightly different forms in all of Tillich's major works.

This suggestion can be approached in a slightly different way by noting the dual fact that no non-human species exhibits religious behaviour and that all human cultures show some behaviour that can be called religious. Thus religion seems to be uniquely human and to derive from that which distinguishes man from the other animals, namely, his self-awareness or capacity for self-transcendence. Because of this self-awareness man can ask certain fundamental existential questions about the ultimate meaning of human life and destiny. Then religion can be defined as the answers which an individual or a group gives to these questions.

A third way of approaching this is to note that man is the being who must make value judgements, decisions about what he should do, decisions about good and evil, about right and wrong, about how he will lead his life. In order to make such decisions with any consistency, a person must have a criterion of good and evil, a standard for his value judgements, a source of order and direction in his life. Such a criterion or standard constitutes the person's religion.[1]

Now it becomes clear that all of these approaches really amount to the same thing. A person's ultimate concern is what determines his answers to the existential questions and what constitutes his standard for value judgements. The relation of this definition of religion to the phenomena traditionally called religions is indicated by the fact that if a particular ultimate concern is adequate and comprehensive enough to attract the allegiance of a considerable number of people, it will tend to develop the cultural forms of a religion in the narrower sense of the word, namely, a cultus, a community organization, a creed, and a code of conduct.

Such a redefinition of religion is formal; it does not specify the object of ultimate concern and thus has the advantage of not limiting religion to allegiance to a personal creator god,

[1] See E. LaB. Cherbonnier, *Hardness of Heart: A Contemporary Interpretation of the Doctrine of Sin* (Garden City: Doubleday and Company, 1955), chs. ii–iv.

for example. Almost every object of human experience has at one time or other been the object of ultimate concern and thus the subject of religion, and this redefinition can cover all such religions.

An important implication of this redefinition is that religion is a universal and unavoidable human phenomenon.

> This means that it is ultimately impossible to avoid religion of some sort. If as existing men we never avoid values or concerns, and if in any human structure of such concerns or values we may always somewhere discover an ultimate concern, then religion will always manifest itself in some way in human existence. It seems thus to be an inevitable part of human existence.[1]

It is interesting to note that in an important recent contribution to the philosophy of religion, Herbert H. Farmer's *Revelation and Religion*, this concept of religion is explicitly rejected.[2] Professor Farmer's thesis is that religion is essentially the personal encounter with and awareness of God as personal. Moreover, the normative concept and essence of religion is revealed once and for all in Christianity, and all other types of religion will manifest the elements which are fundamental to Christianity in varying degrees of completeness and distortion. The result is that various phenomena and beliefs which have been closely associated with religion, such as animism, survival of souls, ancestor worship, totemism, mana, and taboo, are not essentially religious because they do not necessarily involve any relationship to God. This applies also to certain fundamental human needs, such as the need for corporate life, vital power, withdrawal, fulfilment, and integration. These needs can be felt and their satisfaction enjoyed without any relation to religion as Farmer defines it.

---

[1] Hutchison and Martin, op. cit., p. 12, Cf. Walter Marshall Horton, *Christian Theology: An Ecumenical Approach* (New York: Harper and Brothers, 1955), pp. 10–17; John Dewey, *A Common Faith* (New Haven: Yale University Press, 1934), pp. 9f; Emil Brunner, *Christianity and Civilisation: Foundations* (New York: Charles Scribner's Sons, 1948), p. 11.

[2] London: Nisbet and Company, 1954, pp. 166f.

Consequently he rejects the concept of "substitute religion" which suggests that Communism, patriotism, and Comte's "religion of humanity" can be considered religions. Either there is some apprehension of the essential elements of religion or there is not.[1]

There seems, however, to be a contradiction in Farmer's view. On the one hand he states that human nature is constituted by a constant and inescapable personal relationship to God and that God is always pressing in upon man in all the circumstances of his life.[2] Yet on the other hand he can assert that many of the phenomena often associated with religion and many fundamental human needs and their satisfaction may have no relationship to God. Furthermore, his definition of religion seems to imply that all religion is good and that apart from the distorting factor of human sin every religion would tend to become equivalent to Christianity.[3] Consequently it would seem that Farmer's definition of religion is too narrow, and that a broader definition, such as has been suggested above, would be more fruitful in clarifying the meaning of religion and its relation to philosophy. However, the question which Farmer raises is a fundamental one for the Christian philosophy of religion, namely, how is God related to the phenomenon of ultimate concerns?

Our redefinition of religion involves a modification of the meaning of theology. If theology is the systematic explanation of what is believed in any particular religion, then its reference must be expanded to include all ultimate concerns and not simply those that have traditionally been called religions. Furthermore, because a religion or ultimate concern tends to organize and give meaning to all areas of life and experience, theology will tend to become the systematic interpretation of life and experience from the point of view of the ultimate concern. Thus theology will tend to become a world view or *Weltanschauung* based on an ultimate concern.

[1] *Revelation and Religion*, pp. 25ff, 34f, 78f, 84f, 89ff, 163f.
[2] Ibid., pp. 84, 95f.   [3] Ibid., p. 86.

The important fact about philosophy in this connection is that all philosophical systems are based upon a key-category, guiding image, or organizing principle. Every philosophical system is founded on the affirmation of some element in the totality of experience as of supreme significance for the interpretation of the whole. This key-category has been described as a "judgment of importance and significance", an "organizing hypothesis or principle", a "basic analogy or root metaphor", and a "guiding image".

> Like the religious judgments, the basic metaphysical judgments are of the nature of total assertions; they are judgments of importance and significance which govern the development of a theory. If you ask from whence are these basic judgments derived, I should suggest that they are derived predominantly from some particular type of experience, *e.g.* intellectual, aesthetic or moral, which has seemed to provide a clue in terms of which a *Weltanschauung* or philosophical attitude could be developed. The theory must then be developed according to canons of consistency and comprehensiveness; but the basic impetus to the creation of that particular interpretative theory comes from a particular kind of experience which gives rise to a judgment of importance. The basic insight or judgment of importance provides an impulse to achieve some coherent and wider co-ordination of experience with reference to it.[1]

Miss Emmet goes on to indicate the basic judgements of importance made by Plato, Aristotle, Spinoza, Leibniz, Kant, Hegel, Alexander, Whitehead, Bradley, and McTaggart. Areas of experience which have been chosen as the source of

[1] Dorothy M. Emmet, *The Nature of Metaphysical Thinking* (London: Macmillan and Company, 1953), p. 194. Cf. John Herman Randall, Jr, and Justus Buchler, *Philosophy: An Introduction* (New York: Barnes and Noble, 1942), pp. 13f; Stephen C. Pepper, *World Hypotheses: A Study in Evidence* (Berkeley: University of California Press, 1948), ch. v; John Wild, *Human Freedom and Social Order: An Essay in Christian Philosophy* (Durham: Duke University Press, 1959), pp. 3, 90ff, 113ff. This concept is almost identical with that of the "standpoint" and "basic attitude" developed in H. A. Hodges, *Languages, Standpoints and Attitudes* (London: Oxford University Press, 1953), pp. 15f, 50ff.

organizing principles in philosophical systems are mathematics and logic, mechanism or the physical order, organism and evolution, moral experience, economics, mind or spirit. Then on the basis of this choice the philosopher proceeds to interpret the rest of experience. Furthermore, if a philosophical system is to be complete and comprehensive, it must attempt to interpret man's experience of self-awareness and the existential questions which arise from this.

What then is the relation between philosophy and religion so defined? Since a philosopher must have a religion, an ultimate concern to which he gives his allegiance, and since he must deal with the existential questions if his philosophy is to be comprehensive, then it would seem that his religion or ultimate concern would tend to become the key-category or organizing principle of his philosophy. This means that the value or concern which is the source of meaning in his life and to which he gives the highest priority in the decisions of his life would tend to become the principle by which he is best able to interpret and organize all the areas of his experience. Or the reverse might be the case. That principle or area of experience by which a philosopher is best enabled to make a comprehensive and coherent interpretation of the rest of experience would tend to become his ultimate concern, the object of his religious allegiance.[1] This suggestion is subject to historical verification and would be a fruitful approach to the study of the history of philosophy. It would be a "theological history of philosophy".[2]

A problem arises as to the significance of a case in which

---

[1] Cf. John Oman, *The Natural and the Supernatural* (New York: The Macmillan Company, 1931), pp. 149f; John Baillie, *The Interpretation of Religion* (Edinburgh: T. & T. Clark, 1929), pp. 38ff; Herman Dooyeweerd, *A New Critique of Theoretical Thought*, Vol. I: *The Necessary Presuppositions of Philosophy* (Philadelphia: The Presbyterian and Reformed Publishing Company, 1953).

[2] Tillich, *Systematic Theology*, I, pp. 39f. Such a study is under way in Richard Kroner's, *Speculation and Revelation in the History of Philosophy* (Philadelphia: The Westminster Press, 1956–9).

this tendency does not appear, a case in which there is a clear-cut distinction between the ultimate concern and the organizing principle of the philosopher. The case of a naturalistic humanism comes to mind in which the ultimate concern of the philosopher is certain human values whereas his organizing principle is nature. It would seem in this case, and perhaps in other similar cases, that the ultimate concern is not justified by the organizing principle and vice versa. This would indicate an incoherence in the world view in question.

This suggestion can be summarized in the statement that all philosophies have religious foundations and all religions have philosophical implications, or that every philosophy has an existential basis in the ultimate concern of the philosopher, or that every philosopher is a hidden theologian.[1]

If the foregoing analysis is correct, then in the scrutiny and criticism of his organizing principle even the philosopher who is not committed to a religion in the narrower sense will confront the same problem as the philosopher who is so committed. Thus every philosopher faces the problem of trying to combine the attitudes of assurance and inquiry.

Of course, it may be objected that it is no business of the philosopher to try to construct a system or a world view. But the majority of philosophers from the beginning have believed that their task was constructive as well as critical, metaphysical as well as logical. And it has been cogently argued that even the critical function of philosophy presupposes a constructive or metaphysical perspective.

It may also be objected that an empirical or pragmatic approach to the interpretation of experience and existential questions could and should be carried on with as little commitment as possible or no commitment at all, since commitment is detrimental to clear thinking. Then, however, it may be presumed that one should be committed to non-committal inquiry.

---

[1] Hutchison, op. cit., p. 28; Tillich, *Systematic Theology*, I, pp. 24f; *The Protestant Era*, pp. 89f.

I have seen a man get red in the face, roar and pound the table in defense of his belief that dispassionate, scientific objectivity is the only way of getting at the truth—without being conscious in the least of the discrepancy between his actions and his thesis.[1]

It may further be objected that philosophers have not always found it difficult to subject to radical scrutiny the basic presuppositions and organizing principles of their philosophical systems. But the reason for this is probably that academic philosophers have often failed to deal with the existential questions, and this has made it possible for them to keep their organizing principles separate from their ultimate concerns.[2] This means that their systems have not been comprehensive and that their answers to the existential questions are given by implication in their lives and have probably suffered by not being related to their philosophical systems.

There will, of course, be periods in which a philosopher is developing or modifying his organizing principle and his world view. But even during these periods he cannot lead an ordered life or think constructively without an ultimate concern or organizing principle, and his world view will be indicated by the fragments already affirmed and by his life. A philosopher changes his organizing principle and world view or exchanges it for another when he has a new encounter with reality in which new experience is gained which cannot be comprehended or interpreted adequately in the old world view. This is called conversion in the realm traditionally referred to as religious.[3]

Therefore, it seems to be quite misleading when Temple states that, unlike theology, "philosophy starts from the detailed experience of men, and seeks to build up its understanding of that experience by reference to that experience

---

[1] David E. Roberts, *Psychotherapy and a Christian View of Man* (New York: Charles Scribner's Sons, 1950), p. 61n.

[2] See Wild, op. cit., pp. 17f, 135ff, *et passim*.

[3] Hodges, *Languages, Standpoints, and Attitudes*, p. 58.

alone".[1] On the contrary, it must be asserted that philosophy, like theology, starts by looking at the world of experience from the standpoint or perspective of its organizing principle.

It now becomes clear why Temple was not able to carry out the plan of the Gifford Lectures in the way he defined it, namely, without dependence on doctrine accepted on authority or more specifically without dependence on the Christian revelation. Temple may have avoided such dependence in form but not in substance and actuality. The Christian revelation is Temple's organizing principle, and it is not something which can or should be suppressed in his philosophy of religion. It is the unavoidable and indispensable means of accomplishing anything in philosophy. As a result Temple's venture in the philosophy of religion is apologetic in the sense that all constructive philosophical writing is apologetic. Constructive philosophy involves showing how the facts are illuminated by and also support the validity of the organizing principle. This is suggested by Temple is his dictum: "Whatever a man starts by believing, it appears that experience is likely to confirm him in that belief."[2]

Consequently, the tension between philosophy and religion or between critical philosophy and theological philosophy which Temple discusses in lecture ii of *Nature, Man and God* is actually that which exists between different world views based on different organizing principles. It is the same kind of tension which exists, for example, between naturalism and idealism and between Buddhist philosophy and Mohammedan philosophy. Temple suggests this when he asserts that "the province claimed by both [philosophy and religion] is the entire field of human experience".[3]

These considerations lead to a redefinition of the philosophy of religion. It is the department of philosophy which carries on the investigation and interpretation of ultimate concerns and the world views based on them from the perspective of the

---

[1] *Nature, Man and God.* p. 45.   [2] Ibid., p. 278.   [3] Ibid., p. 31.

organizing principle chosen by the philosopher. It will include the interpretation of the anthropological, sociological, psychological, and historical data concerning the various religions, and in the final stages it will involve judgements on the validity or truth of the religions.

A special problem arises here as to whether the philosopher includes his own ultimate concern under the general category of religion. If he does,[1] then his philosophy of religion is the interpretation of religion including his own in so far as it falls within the general class of religion but not in so far as it is normative for him. (This would be his theology.) But he may also choose to exclude his own religion from the investigation,[2] and then his philosophy of religion is the interpretation of religions other than his own. This problem is raised by the possibility of distinguishing between a religion seen empirically and its transcendent norm.

Consequently, there will not be one body of knowledge known as the philosophy of religion, but there will be as many philosophies of religion as there are philosophies or organizing principles and world views based on them.[3] There is, for example, a naturalistic philosophy of religion[4] and a Christian philosophy of religion.[5] But when a Christian philosopher examines Christianity in so far as it is normative for

[1] See, for example, Farmer, op. cit., pp. 30–41.

[2] See, for example, Brunner, *Revelation and Reason*, pp. 258, 272.

[3] A. Seth Pringle-Pattison, *Studies in the Philosophy of Religion* (Oxford: The Clarendon Press, 1930), p. 8.

[4] See, for example, John Herman Randall, Jr. "The Meaning of Religion for Man", *Preface to Philosophy: Textbook*, ed. William Pearson Tolley (New York: The Macmillan Company, 1947); Sterling P. Lamprecht, "Naturalism and Religion", *Naturalism and the Human Spirit*, ed. Yervant H. Krikorian; George Santayana, *Reason in Religion* (New York: Charles Scribner's Sons, 1936).

[5] See, for example, Hendrick Kraemer, *The Christian Message in a Non-Christian World* (New York: International Missionary Council, 1947), chs. iv–vi; *Religion and the Christian Faith* (London: Lutterworth Press, 1956); Brunner, *Revelation and Reason*, chs. xv–xvii; Tillich, *Systematic Theology*, I, pp. 211–35; Edward J. Jurji, *The Christian Interpretation of Religion* (New York: The Macmillan Company, 1952); Farmer, op cit.

him, the result is Christian theology, the articulation of the
Christian organizing principle. Likewise when a naturalistic
philosopher examines naturalism, the result is the central
philosophy or "theology" of naturalism, the articulation of
the naturalistic organizing principle.

When religion is redefined as ultimate concern which is
potentially and can become actually an organizing principle
for a metaphysic or world view, the philosophy of religion
becomes crucially important for philosophy and in fact the
central task of philosophy. If the constructive task of philosophy is to develop a comprehensive and coherent world
view on the basis of an ultimate concern or organizing principle, then a critical and comparative study of ultimate concerns will be an essential and fundamental step in this task.
If an ultimate concern is the necessary foundation and impulse
for the development of a world view, then the main business
of philosophy will be the interpretation of the phenomenon
of ultimate concerns and the world views based on them or
the philosophy of religion. Thus, Dilthey believed the philosopher's real task to be such a "philosophy of philosophy",
a comparative and critical *Weltanschauungslehre*.[1]

An important result of this redefinition of religion and its
relation to philosophy is that theology and philosophy come
to be seen as parallel enterprises.[2] Both theology and philosophy are attempts to organize and interpret all areas of
human experience on the basis of some ultimate concern or
organizing principle. This is indicated by a fact that has been
noted above. When a philosopher or a school of philosophers
develops a comprehensive world view, a coherent synthesis

[1] Hodges, *Wilhelm Dilthey: An Introduction* (London: Routledge and
Kegan Paul, 1944), p. 99.
[2] Cf. Tillich, *The Protestant Era*, pp. 88f; *Systematic Theology*, I, pp. 24f;
Emmet, *The Nature of Metaphysical Thinking*, pp. 150f; R. G. Collingwood,
Religion and Philosophy (London: Macmillan and Company, Ltd, 1916),
pp. 16ff; M. B. Foster, " 'We' in Modern Philosophy", *Faith and Logic*,
ed. Basil Mitchell (Boston: The Beacon Press, 1957), pp. 213, 219f.

which deals with all the existential questions and which is adequate enough to gain any degree of acceptance, it will tend to develop a cult community similar to the philosophical schools of the Hellenistic period.[1] In other words it will tend to function as a religion for those who affirm it. Something like this can be seen in connection with contemporary naturalistic humanism.[2]

Temple implies the parallelism of theology and philosophy when he points out that the province claimed by both is the entire field of human experience and that a perfect theology and a perfect philosophy would coincide.[3] His fundamental disagreement with this idea is based on what he believed to be their difference in method, and it is the investigation of this point which has led us to the parallelism of theology and philosophy.

It may be objected that the essence of philosophy is a continuous search for an adequate organizing principle, whereas theology has decided on this from the beginning. Thus, Edwin A. Burtt, for example, states:

> The theologian is essentially a teacher, presenting to others a detailed and logically persuasive defense of his major convictions after he has reached them; while the philosopher of religion, as such, is essentially an inquirer, ready to share with other inquirers the process of exploration by which he fumbles his way toward such convictions as he may ultimately reach. Of course, when he reaches them he may become an instructor too, and proffer a theology.[4]

[1] W. H. V. Reade, *The Christian Challenge to Philosophy* (London: S.P.C.K., 1951), ch. 1.

[2] See, for example, Roy Wood Sellars, "Naturalistic Humanism", *Religion in the Twentieth Century*, ed. Vergilius Ferm (New York: The Philosophical Library, 1948); John Herman Randall, Jr, "Naturalistic Humanism", *Patterns of Faith in America Today*, ed. F. Ernest Johnson (New York: Harper and Brothers, 1957); John Dewey, *A Common Faith* (New Haven: Yale University Press, 1934); Julian Huxley, *Religion Without Revelation* (New York: Harper and Brothers, 1957).

[3] *Nature, Man and God*, pp. 30f, 474; *Mens Creatrix*, p. 3.

[4] *Types of Religious Philosophy* (New York: Harper and Brothers, 1939), p. 9.

There may be periods in the lives of individual philosophers during which they are actually searching for an organizing principle, but almost all philosophical writing with a few important exceptions, such as some of the Platonic dialogues, has been the interpretation of experience by means of an organizing principle which has been accepted and which receives added support by the adequacy of the interpretations based upon it. Furthermore, the search for an organizing principle is not carried on by someone who has none, because, as we have seen, it is impossible to live without some kind of ultimate concern or potential organizing principle no matter how inchoate or unconsciously held.

> [Dilthey] has seen the psychological necessity of a *Weltanschauung* to give unity and direction to a life, and it is obvious that a *Weltanschauung* can only do this if it is not merely toyed with, but definitely held. And that means that its rivals must be definitely not held, i.e., must be rejected. It is possible to play with rival points of view, manipulating them like a juggler, so long only as we have not to live and act in earnest, but in times of stress and danger or in moments of responsibility this is not possible. In such times, *if not always,* we see that points of view, *Weltanschauungen,* are not merely to be studied and enjoyed, but to be held and acted on, and for that purpose we want not many points of view, but one. If philosophy, or rather life itself, confronts us with many rival views of things, then we must take one and reject the rest. . . . It is always possible . . . to synthesize ideas, or to hold diverse points of view together, so long as we are standing aloof, as spectators, and studying them. When it comes to holding them and acting on them, the oppositions reassert themselves, and we find that we cannot take sides with one without taking sides against another. To live is to act, and to act is to choose, and to choose is also to reject.[1]

It may also be objected that theology is simply the systematic articulation of the organizing principle or fundamental doctrines of a religion and is not as comprehensive as philosophy should be. It is true that Christian theology, for example,

---

[1] Hodges, *Wilhelm Dilthey: An Introduction,* p. 105, italics added.

has more often than not been interpreted in this rather restricted manner.[1] It has traditionally been understood to be a systematic interpretation of the central doctrines of the Christian faith with perhaps additional sections on ethics and apologetics. Often the section on ethics has dealt with the interpretation of general moral experience and problems of politics and economics, and the section on apologetics has dealt with the interpretation of non-Christian religions, philosophy, and science. But rarely has Christian theology addressed itself to the interpretation of such areas of human experience as aesthetics, logic, language, and culture as a whole. Increasingly, however, in the past generation Christian theology has become aware of its larger task of attempting to interpret all areas of experience.[2] This larger task has been referred to quite properly as Christian philosophy to indicate its difference from the traditional conception of the scope of Christian theology.

> The Faith must seek to understand itself, but it is equally, if subsequently, true that it must then go on to understand everything else by interpreting reality in terms of its own vision and from its own standpoint.[3]

The objections to the parallel character of philosophy and theology have been most forcefully stated by Paul Tillich.[4] He

[1] See, for example, Arnold S. Nash, *The University and the Modern World: An Essay in the Philosophy of University Education* (New York: The Macmillan Company, 1943), pp. 289ff.

[2] See, for example, Tillich, *The Religious Situation*, trans. H. R. Neibuhr (New York: Henry Holt and Company, 1932); and *The Protestant Era*; Brunner, *Christianity and Civilization*; Richard Kroner, *Culture and Faith* (Chicago: The University of Chicago Press, 1951). It will be noted below that Temple's major works are in fact Christian philosophy.

[3] Casserley, op. cit., p. 252. Cf. Alan Richardson, *Christian Apologetics* (New York: Harper and Brothers, 1947), pp. 38f; George F. Thomas (ed.), *The Vitality of the Christian Tradition* (New York: Harper and Brothers, 1944), pp. 251–65; Brunner, *Revelation and Reason*, ch. xxv; Nash, op. cit., ch. vii; Leonard Hodgson, *Towards a Christian Philosophy* (London: Nisbet and Company, 1944); Farmer, op. cit., pp. 16ff; Wild, op. cit., pp. 3–5, 91–152.

[4] *The Protestant Era*, pp. 88ff; *Systematic Theology*, I, pp. 22ff.

asserts that philosophy and theology diverge in their cognitive attitude, in the difference of their sources, and in the difference of their content. Philosophy is basically theoretical while theology is basically existential. Philosophy abstracts from the existential situation while theology is bound to it. There seem to be contradictions in his view of this problem, and they have been ably pointed out by his critics.[1] In response to these criticisms Tillich has granted "a basic identity of theology and philosophy" and asserted that "the eschatological unity of theology and philosophy must also have a present actuality, however fragmentary".[2] In any case the divergences between philosophy and theology indicated by Tillich seem to point to differences in ultimate concern, organizing principle, and world view rather than to differences between the two disciplines as such.

Another objection to the parallelism of philosophy and theology is that there are certain problems which are purely philosophical, with which theology is not at all concerned and to which theology is irrelevant. Thus it is concluded that philosophy and theology cannot be parallel because they deal at least in part with distinct problems. Examples that have been offered of such problems are certain questions in logic and epistemology, the mind-body problem, and the issue between nominalism and realism. However, if logical statements imply or presuppose metaphysical statements and if theology represents at least a potential metaphysic, then it would seem that the elaboration of the theological world view would at the very least severely limit or narrow down the possibilities of an answer to any philosophical problem. That an analysis from the point of view of Christian theology can illuminate many of the classical philosophical problems has been indicated, for example, in J. V. L. Casserley's *The*

[1] Charles W. Kegley and Robert W. Bretall (eds.), *The Theology of Paul Tillich* (New York: The Macmillan Company, 1952), pp. 100ff, 113f, 140, 200ff.
[2] Kegley and Bretall, op. cit., p. 336.

Christian in Philosophy and in Paul Tillich's *Systematic Theology*. Casserley demonstrates that the perspective of Christian theology can shed considerable light on the problems of the singular, language, and history. Tillich demonstrates the same in regard to many of the traditional problems of ontology.

A final objection to the parallel character of philosophy and theology takes the form of the denial of the possibility of a Christian philosophy. It is often pointed out, for example, that Christian theology is dependent upon philosophy in that it cannot formulate its central categories without borrowing concepts which have been produced and refined in the philosophical tradition. But this is certainly also true of idealism, naturalism, existentialism, and logical empiricism. The Christian philosopher as well as the non-Christian philosopher must use the concepts of the philosophical tradition or develop his own concepts and test them in the philosophical market-place. The philosophical tradition, however, is not a source of concepts which is foreign to the Christian tradition, since the latter itself has often been the source of philosophical concepts and has almost always been deeply determinative in the development of the philosophical tradition.[1]

Tillich's objections to the idea of a Christian philosophy are not to the project which has been described above. He rejects a Christian philosophy which is either a canonization of a past philosopher or which is based on a demand that contemporary philosophers intentionally limit themselves to predetermined limits and goals. He does not reject the possibility of a philosopher who is a Christian attempting freely to interpret experience on the existential basis of his ultimate concern in the same way that every philosopher must attempt it. In fact he has more recently stated in an unpublished lecture: "You are a Christian philosopher when you are a Christian and philosophize."

[1] See, for example, Casserley, op. cit., pp. 256–9; Brunner, *Revelation and Reason*, p. 375.

In summary, what we find in the philosophical-theological enterprise is a variety of world views of varying completeness. Some of these world views have traditionally been called religious, some have been called philosophical, and some have not been clearly formulated. Some are near to others, some overlap, and some are in complete contradiction to others. Each is based on an ultimate concern, key-category, or organizing principle by which the various areas of experience are interpreted. The wider the acceptance of a world view, the more it will tend to become like the phenomena traditionally called religions. It is possible for a person to exchange one world view for another, but it is impossible to avoid commitment to some world view, although this commitment may be inchoate and by implication. The conflict between philosophy and theology is really a conflict between different world views and is parallel to that between different philosophies or different theologies. A person's examination of his ultimate concern or organizing principle may be called his central philosophy or theology. His interpretation of the other realms of experience on the basis of his organizing principle can be called his philosophy. His investigation of other world views and the ultimate concerns on which they are based will be the part of his philosophy called the philosophy of religion. Within this there will be a narrower study, the interpretation of the phenomena traditionally known as religions.

When understood in this way the philosophy of religion and theology can make real contributions to contemporary philosophy and vice versa. As in the first centuries of the Christian era so to-day it is clear that philosophy and theology need each other and become poor when they are separated.[1]

It is a commonplace, but nonetheless true in large measure, that much of contemporary philosophy has ceased to deal

[1] Cf. Casserley, op. cit., p. 23; Tillich, *The Protestant Era*, p. 89; George F. Thomas, "The Philosophy of Religion", *Protestant Thought in the Twentieth Century: Whence and Whither?*, ed. Arnold S. Nash (New York: The Macmillan Company, 1951), pp. 98f; Hutchison, op. cit., pp. 4, 29.

fruitfully with what have been traditionally understood to be the central and perennial problems of philosophy. Concern with methodology has often displaced concern with metaphysical problems and existential questions. Theology and the philosophy of religion should be able to contribute to contemporary philosophy new themes and problems, a new stimulus and vision of the possibilities of its constructive function.

On the other hand, much of contemporary theology and philosophy of religion, both in their liberal and their neoorthodox forms, is fuzzy, uncritical, and apparently contemptuous of precision, clarity, consistency, and coherence. If contemporary philosophy has often failed in its constructive function, then certainly contemporary theology and philosophy of religion have often failed in their critical function. Contemporary philosophy should be able to remind theology and philosophy of religion that they are inevitably involved in problems of logic and epistemology. The theologian especially must learn to relate his own special categories to those of the philosophical tradition. Theology, if it is to be true to its task, must learn to become self-critical, rational in its own proper sense, precise in its use of terms, coherent in its statements, and consistent in its wholeness.

In the light of this analysis it now becomes clear that Temple's three major works, *Mens Creatrix*, *Christ the Truth*, and *Nature, Man and God*, are really Christian philosophy cast in an apologetic form.[1] They are not primarily Christian philosophy of religion since the interpretation of religious phenomena is not their primary purpose. In these works Temple investigates and interprets from the perspective of the Christian organizing principle almost every area of human experience: intellectual experience, logic, epistemology, time, value, art, tragedy, conduct and moral experience, society, liberty, education, internationalism, religion, the problem of evil, and history.

---

[1] Charles W. Lowry describes Temple as a "Christian Philosopher" in "William Temple—Thinker, Theologian", *Christendom*, X (Winter, 1945), p. 7.

But in each case he casts his investigations in the form of an argument for the validity, adequacy, and truth of the Christian world view.

In *Mens Creatrix* he makes a philosophical analysis of the four main areas of human experience: knowledge, art, morality, and religion, and shows that they present four converging lines which do not meet. Then he shows that the Christian hypothesis supplies the central point at which the four converging lines can meet in a coherent world view. In *Christ the Truth* Temple states that his aim is to present a Christocentric metaphysics. This he attempts to do again by examining the major metaphysical questions, the central Christian affirmations, and finally re-examining the metaphysical questions in the light of the Christian faith. Only one quarter of the Gifford Lectures is devoted to the dialectical argument for theism. The other fifteen lectures are related to this argument but are primarily examples of Christian philosophy: the investigation from the Christian point of view of the major philosophical problems of logic, value, freedom, religious experience, evil, and history.

In his power as a Christian philosopher, William Temple has few equals in this generation in breadth of comprehension and in depth of insight. As Christian theology takes up again its larger task, Temple's contribution to Christian philosophy will come into its own.

BIBLIOGRAPHY

The following lists are not complete but include only those writings by William Temple which bear directly on his philosophy of religion. A date in parentheses after the date of publication is the date of first publication.

1. Books and Parts of Books by William Temple

The Centrality of Christ. New York: Morehouse Publishing Company, 1936.

Christ the Truth. New York: The Macmillan Company, 1924.

"Chairman's Introduction", *Doctrine in the Church of England*. London: S.P.C.K., 1938. Pp. 1–18.

Christian Faith and Life. New York: The Macmillan Company, 1936 (1931).

Christianity and Social Order. New York: Penguin Books Inc., 1942.

Christianity as an Interpretation of History. London: Longmans, Green and Company, 1945.

Christianity in Thought and Practice. New York: Morehouse Publishing Company, 1936.

The Church and Its Teaching Today. New York: The Macmillan Company, 1936.

"The Divinity of Christ", *Foundations: A Statement of Christian Belief in Terms of Modern Thought*. London: Macmillan and Company, Ltd, 1913 (1912). Pp. 211–63.

The Faith and Modern Thought. London: Macmillan and Company, Ltd., 1924 (1910).

Fellowship with God. London: Macmillan and Company, Ltd, 1920.

The Kingdom of God. London: Macmillan and Company, Ltd, 1913 (1912).

Mens Creatrix. London: Macmillan and Company, Ltd, 1917.

Nature, Man and God. London: Macmillan and Company, Ltd, 1951 (1934).

The Nature of Personality. London: Macmillan and Company, Ltd, 1911.

Personal Religion and the Life of Fellowship. London: Longmans, Green and Company, 1926.

Plato and Christianity. London: Macmillan and Company, Ltd, 1916.

Religious Experience and Other Essays and Addresses. Ed. A. E. Baker. London: James Clarke and Company, 1958. (This collection includes "Christianity as an Interpretation of History" listed above and "What Christians Stand For in the Secular World" listed below.)

Revelation. Ed. John Baillie and Hugh Martin. New York: The Macmillan Company, 1937. Pp. 83–123.

"Some Implications of Theism", *Contemporary British Philosophy: Personal Statements* (First Series). Ed. John H. Muirhead. New York: The Macmillan Company, 1924. Pp. 411–28.

Studies in the Spirit and Truth of Christianity. London: Macmillan and Company, Ltd, 1914.

Thoughts in War-Time. London: Macmillan and Company, Ltd, 1940.

The Universality of Christ. London: S.C.M., 1921.

2. *Periodical Articles by William Temple*

"Christians in the Secular World", *The Christian Century*, LXI (1 March 1944), pp. 269–71.

"Christianity as a Historical Religion", *Theology*, XXXII (January 1936), pp. 8–17.

"How Can We Find God?", *The Christian Century*, XLVI (28 February 1929), pp. 291–2.

"The Idea of God", *The Spectator*, CXLVI (4 April 1931), pp. 537–8.

"The Love of God our Hope of Immortality", *The Hibbert Journal*, XIV (April 1916), pp. 538–50.

"Plato's Vision of the Ideas", *Mind*, N.S. XVII (October 1908), pp. 502–17.

"Unitarianism and the Gospel", *The Moslem World*, XXV (December 1935), pp. 1–3.

"The Value of Philosophy to Religion", *The Journal of Philosophical Studies*, III (July 1928), pp. 345–8.

"What Christians Stand for in the Secular World", *The Christian News-Letter*, Supplement to No. 198 (29 December 1943), pp. 1–12.

3. *Books and Articles about William Temple*

Baker, A. E. (ed.). *William Temple's Teaching*. London: James Clarke and Company, n.d.

Bennett, John C. "William Temple", *Anglican Theological Review*, XXV (July 1943), pp. 257–71.

Harris, Edward G. "Some Basic Notions in the Philosophy of Religion of William Temple, Archbishop of Canterbury." Unpublished Master's Thesis, Union Theological Seminary, New York, 1945.

Iremonger, F. A. *William Temple, Archbishop of Canterbury: His Life and Letters.* London: Oxford University Press, 1948.

Lowry, Charles W., Jr. "William Temple: Archbishop of Canterbury", *Christendom*, VIII (Winter 1943), pp. 26–41.

——. "William Temple—Thinker, Theologian", *Christendom*, X (Winter 1945), pp. 5–8.

Matthews, W. R., *et al. William Temple: An Estimate and An Appreciation.* London: James Clarke and Company, 1946.

Miller, Randolph Crump. "Is Temple a Realist?", *The Journal of Religion*, XIX (January 1939), pp. 44–54.

4. *Reviews of William Temple's Major Works:*
Mens Creatrix

Anonymous. *The Church Quarterly Review*, LXXXIV (July 1917), pp. 356–8.

Brightman, E. S. *The Philosophical Review*, XXVII (March 1918), pp. 210–12.

Galloway, G. *The Hibbert Journal*, XV (July 1917), pp. 689–92.

Miller, Dickinson S. "Mr. Temple and Anglican Thought", *Anglican Theological Review*, I (March 1919), pp. 407–25.

Taylor, A. E. *Mind*, N.S. XXVII (April 1918), pp. 208–34.

Christ the Truth

Anonymous. *Theology*, X (February 1925), pp. 61–3.

Pryke, W. Maurice. *The Modern Churchman*, XV (April and May 1925), pp. 73–6.

Tennant, F. R. *The Journal of Theological Studies*, XXVI (April 1925), pp. 295–8.

Widgery, Alban G. *The Hibbert Journal*, XXIII (April 1925), pp. 559–61.

Youtz, H. A. *The Journal of Religion*, V (May 1925), pp. 327–9.

Nature, Man and God

Aubrey, Edwin Ewart. *The Journal of Religion*, XVI (January 1936), pp. 100–3.

Edwards, E. W. *Mind*, N.S. XLIV (April 1935), pp. 240–2.

Evans, Daniel. *Christendom*, I (October 1935), pp. 181–4.

Goudge, H. L. "Some Modern Teaching on Freedom", *The Church Quarterly Review*, CXXII (April 1936), pp. 1–18.

Groves, C. P. *The London Quarterly Review*, CLX (January 1935), pp. 90–3.

Kirk, K. E. *The Church Quarterly Review*, CXX (July 1935), pp. 301–8.

Smith, J. S. Boys. "A New Apologetic", *The Modern Churchman*, XXV (April 1935), pp. 7–14.

Stedman, Ralph E. *The Hibbert Journal*, XXXIII (January 1935), pp. 301–5.

Tennant, F. R. *The Journal of Theological Studies*, XXXVI (July 1935), pp. 313–16.

Tremenheere, G. H. *Theology*, XXXI (November 1935), pp. 285–6.

Turner, J. E. *Theology*, XXX (April 1935). pp. 243–7.

Webb, C. C. J. *Philosophy*, X (April 1935), pp. 225–8.

INDEX